WE NEED TO TALK

WE NEED TO TALK

STEPHEN and CHRIS
from GOGGLEBOX

HEADLINE

First published in 2016
by HEADLINE PUBLISHING GROUP

1

Cataloguing in Publication Data is available from the British Library

Hardback ISBN 978 1 4722 4386 7

Typeset in Berling by Palimpsest Book Production Limited, Falkirk, Stirlingshire

Printed and bound in the UK by Clays Ltd, St Ives plc

HEADLINE PUBLISHING GROUP
An Hachette UK Company
Carmelite House
50 Victoria Embankment
London EC4 0DZ

www.headline.co.uk
www.hachette.co.uk

Stephen: I'd like to dedicate this book to my mum, Pat, my sisters Denise, Sharon and Beverley and my 'famous five' friends, Kerry, Lorna, Melissa, Madlen and Lee, who have all shaped me in one way or another during the many years I've known them. And to Daniel, whose love and support makes my life just perfect! And to Chris: we both know I'm the funny one, bitch.

Chris: I want to dedicate this book to my incredible parents, Doreen and Jack, for bringing me into the world. Marie and Sharon, the two greatest sisters anyone can have, and the rest of my crazy, brilliant family. To Tony, my wonderful, supportive, kind, handsome fiancé for always being there and taking such good care of Freddie, Rusty, Buddy, Sherbie and I. All my fantastic friends, past and present, for making me who I am today. And finally, Stephen. You couldn't have done this without me.

CONTENTS

WELCOME!

STEPHEN

Fucking hell, Chris, we've written a book. A whole book.

CHRIS

I know! I really hope people like it. There are so many bits I love. Obviously the carrot story is a highlight.

STEPHEN

Obviously. There would be no book without the carrot story. Weirdly, I learnt a lot about you while we were writing it. I thought I know pretty much everything there is to know. You're not exactly shy.

CHRIS

I've got hidden depths. We've both been through quite a lot and I don't know about you, but for me it feels really good to get my story out there. We've been very honest. Maybe too honest in parts. But you only live once, don't you?

STEPHEN

Exactly. If you're going to write a book you may as well do it properly and not hold anything back. Although I'm not sure you should have told everyone that cider story. . .

Chapter One

HEELS OF DREAMS

Stephen: 'Going to the allotment was something we'd look forward to. Especially when it got dark and we used to nick everyone's vegetables.'

STEPHEN

I grew up in Sittingbourne, a town in north Kent. To be honest, not an awful lot happens there. I was born in the front bedroom of our little terrace house in Harold Road, and I was the only one of my siblings to be born at home.

Mum had already had two kids, Denise and Paul, when I came along. Paul was born on 14 July 1970, and I was born on 26 July 1971, so we were ridiculously close together and probably explains why my mum was eight months pregnant before she even realized she was having another baby. She went to her doctor and said, 'I can't lose any weight,' and he replied, 'That's because you're pregnant again.' She was a bit like, 'Oh, for fuck's sake. I've already got *two*.'

I'm convinced that's the reason I've got such a flat head now. My mum had just been through pregnancy and giving birth twice and then I came along by surprise and I think she was bored of the whole thing. I think she used to leave me in my cot all day and wander past every now and again to make sure I was okay or tell me to stop crying, and I think all that lying down gave me a weird shaped head.

CHRIS

The poor cow probably had postnatal depression already, and then she had to deal with you on top of everything else.

STEPHEN

She probably did, to be fair. And then old flathead here comes along.

My mum was quite strict and all we ever heard when we were kids was 'shut up'. My cousin Janette swears she thought her name was 'shut up' for the first five years of her life. I spent a lot of time with my cousins growing up.

My sister Sharon came along a few years later and by that time the rest of us kids were in school and nursery so at least that made things a bit easier on mum. Then my dad left when Sharon was two, I was five, Paul was six and Denise was eight. He literally just fucked off over to Holland, shacked up with some woman and never came home.

I did go and visit my dad a couple of times. The first time I went I was about seven and he already had two more kids. He's got six more in total now.

Mum used to have to take us all the way to France on a ferry and he'd drive down from Holland to collect us. Whenever we went I felt miserable because I always wanted to stay with my mum.

Dad had been in the middle of renovating our house so the downstairs was completely gutted and there wasn't a staircase going to the top floor, so we had to use a ladder to get up and down. I remember that really clearly.

There were two bedrooms right opposite each other and Paul and Denise used to love jumping back and forth into the doorways. One day I was standing in one of the rooms watching them and they told me I had to jump but I was absolutely terrified. Eventually I built up the courage to give it a go, but when I finally leapt across Paul closed the other door and I fell all the way to the ground floor and broke my leg.

Because the house was in such a state and we had no money coming in, it got to the point where mum couldn't pay the mortgage so we got evicted. We moved into a really dodgy council estate called Eagle's Close, which thankfully is being knocked down now. It was rough as arseholes and one of my first memories is of walking down the road with Paul, Denise and Janette and turning a corner into the estate that was going to be our new home. There was a burnt-out car and rubbish strewn everywhere. The unmarried mothers' home was two doors up from us and even at that young age I remember thinking, 'that's where the naughty girls live'.

It was such a horrible place that for the first six months mum didn't let us go out of the house apart from to go to school. Then one day she'd clearly had enough of us hanging round all the time and she said, 'We're not going anywhere so you've just got to get out there and learn to defend yourselves.' And that was it. We were on our own, and I wasn't the toughest little boy in the world.

Mum met another man called John a few years later and they had my sister, Beverley, but their relationship didn't last long. So there was my mum with five kids and no man to help bring us up. What a fucking nightmare.

CHRIS
But from what you've told me in the past you all really pulled together?

STEPHEN
We did when we needed to. But even though Paul and I were really close in age we didn't get on *at all*. We shared a room and I was always moving the furniture around to make the room look prettier. My mum used to do it with our living room so I must have picked it up from her. I still do it in the salon now.

But one day, I went downstairs and I said to my mum, 'Can I move in with the girls?' She took a long drag on her fag, shrugged and said, 'Yeah.' So I moved into my sisters' bedroom and that was much more fun.

CHRIS

You're mad. I would never have *asked* to move in with my sisters.

STEPHEN

Our favourite game to play was 'Pat and Jill'. My mum is called Pat and Jill was our nextdoor neighbour. We'd dress up and put jumpers on our heads so they looked like wigs. Then we'd pretend to be my mum and her mate. We'd do that for hours and we bloody loved it. We'd repeat whatever we'd heard Pat and Jill talk about. For instance, 'Jill' would say, 'Well, Brian didn't come home again last night,' and 'Pat' would whisper angrily, 'Baaaaastard.'

CHRIS

I did a similar thing growing up. My sisters and I had a game called. . . Sisters.

STEPHEN

Imaginative.

CHRIS

Can you guess what it was about? Stephen and I had quite a similar upbringing in a lot of ways. I grew up in a place called Chesham, which was also a shithole. My family – my mum Doreen, my dad Jack, my younger sister Sharon and my older sister Marie – lived in the cemetery lodge because my dad was a gravedigger. This was back in the days when they used to dig holes by hand as well.

STEPHEN

When Chris first told me about his dad I shouted, 'Fuck off!' and started singing the theme tune to *The Addams Family*. It still makes me piss myself now.

CHRIS

We lived in this flint house on the edge of the cemetery, and not surprisingly it was really haunted. We used to see ghosts all the time. This man used to float out of the loft and stand at the end of my bed staring at me. Then he'd turn around and go and look at my little sister Sharon in the cot. She was only about three at the time but even now she clearly remembers this man looking through the bars at her.

STEPHEN

I've never seen a ghost so I can't say I don't believe in them, but I'm still not sure I do.

HEELS OF DREAMS

CHRIS

Well, this shit happened. We stayed in that house until I was five and then my dad decided he didn't want to dig graves anymore. The house came with the job, which obviously meant we had to move. He got a job at the *Bucks Examiner*, which is a local paper, and became a printer.

We moved into a council estate nearby, but unlike Stephen's one it was lovely with loads of trees and everyone looked after their gardens. A lot of the houses had been sold off privately, but then the council started buying them back and moving people in from the horrible estate over the other end of Chesham and it went really downhill. You don't have nice green lawns there now; you have washing machines in people's front gardens.

STEPHEN

You know places are dodgy when people keep their white goods in their front gardens.

CHRIS

And a burnt-out car or two kind of ruins the ambience. The best thing about moving to the estate was that I had my own room. The cemetery lodge was only a two-bedroomed house so I'd shared with Sharon and Marie. Having my own space was amazing. They were so much messier than me, and I had much better taste in home furnishings.

It also meant I kind of had two bedrooms because I always

thought that what was theirs was mine. I used to sneak in and play with their dolls when they weren't around. Stephen was lucky that he had a brother because he had a bit of male influence but I grew up playing with Sindys and Barbies. Sindy was always so much better than Barbie. She was much more flexible and she always ended up with Ken because her legs spread. Barbie's legs were locked.

I never had an Action Man because they didn't appeal to me but I loved all the female dolls. I also loved make-up and shoes. I was reminiscing with some friends the other day and they said to me, 'Chris, we knew you were gay. You were the most coordinated one out of all of us. Your jumper always matched your shoes.'

Sharon had this black leotard that I *loved*. I used to wear it all the time and I loved the fact that when I put it on my willy disappeared. I used to spin around their room wearing it singing this song I'd made up which went, 'Aeroplane, aeroplane, why are you flying?' I think I thought I was a ballerina.

Even though I didn't want to be in the same bedroom as them I missed my sisters and I still wanted to hang out with them all the time. That's when we made up our cleverly named game, Sisters.

Sisters basically involved us nicking my mum's clothes and make-up and dolling ourselves up as if we were going out. And that was it. *That* was the game. I always insisted on being the prettiest sister, which made Sharon and Marie really angry. But I left them with had no choice because I refused to play unless I got to wear the nicest outfit.

I used to get cross if my sisters didn't do their make-up very well because I felt like I was a bit of a natural with that kind of thing. That kind of set the tone for my later years. . .!

When Marie got a bit older she didn't want to play with Sharon and me anymore so we were together constantly. One of our favourite things to do was play Tarzan and Jane in the bath. Sharon was always Tarzan and I was Jane. My job as Jane was to stay at home and make dinner and I'd be sat in the bath swirling the water around and pretending to cook while Sharon would be swinging from the shower rail making Tarzan noises. Every time we played she'd say to me, 'When can I be Jane?' and I'd shout, 'NEVER!' I was quite possessive about that role.

We had a big grassy area out the front of the house and we used to play on there every day. We'd do roly-polys down it and play schools and all sorts. All the other kids on the estate used to come and hang out there.

Then one day we came home to find that my dad had dug up the entire garden and planted dahlias. So we lost our playground. Everyone used to say how amazing dad's dahlias were and we were *furious* about them.

The dahlias were really prone to earwigs so my dad used to attach canes to them all and then hang pots with straws in to catch all the earwigs. Every night my dad would shake the pots out and we'd have to stamp on the earwigs to try and kill them. I hated them. I also developed a massive fear of spiders as a kid, which I still have now. I have to check behind the curtains before I pull them and I won't have windows open at night time in case any crawl in. It's especially perilous because I live in a bungalow. My mum is so scared of them she blocks up all the sinks in her house.

My fear started when I was four. We had an old shed in the garden of Cemetery Lodge that was full of spiders' webs. Often flies would get caught in them because my dad's fishing maggots would hatch, and my dad said it was like *Wacky Races* trying to see which of the spiders would get to the fly first. Back then I thought spiders were funny, but that soon changed.

Marie and I decided to go out into our shed and jump out to scare our dad when he came in. But he didn't realize we were in there so he shut the shed door and we were trapped in there in the pitch black with a load of spiders. We were screaming our heads off and ever since then we've been terrified.

When I was a teenager my dad and Sharon once pretended they were going to get a baby tarantula as a pet and I threatened to move out. By the time they came back I had my bags packed ready to go. Then they broke the news it was a 'hilarious' joke.

Even though it wasn't the prettiest place you've ever seen, everyone on my estate really looked out for each other. It was a real community.

STEPHEN

It was the same with mine. We were all in the same boat and none of us had a pot to piss in so we made everything as special for each other as we could, and we'd help out wherever possible.

I was aware I didn't have much and I felt a bit sad about it, but what we all lacked in material possessions my mum made up for in love. We always felt loved.

CHRIS

We didn't have a lot but everything felt special. I remember getting these little boxes of Mr Men jigsaw puzzles as gifts. Kids would look at them these days and think, 'Where's my iPhone?' But, like Stephen's mum, mine gave us so much love. And we all talked and had fun together. These days, children are sat down in front of an iPad and left to their own devices. You see families out together and everyone's on their phones. People don't have proper conversations anymore.

It's ridiculous what kids have these days with all their gadgets.

STEPHEN

We used to play with a bit of wood or something.

CHRIS

My friend Fred Collins had an Atari computer and all it did was beep over and over again. I remember getting someone's second-hand Commodore 64. You had to put cassettes in it and then wait five minutes for it to load. Then at the last minute it would bloody crash. I got given another hand-me-down, a Commodore 128, and that did exactly the same.

STEPHEN

I can remember getting a radio for Christmas one year and being over the fucking moon with it. I used to sit in my room for hours listening to it, and I used to carry it about with me everywhere. It had a massive square battery and it was bloody heavy. I thought it was the best thing in the world.

CHRIS

I remember when my sisters and I got a cassette player and I used to sit and listen to the Top Ten every Sunday and try and record all the songs. I'd push record as soon as the DJ stopped talking, and then stop it before he started again. But I'd always get a little bit of him speaking no matter how hard I tried to get it right.

STEPHEN

I did exactly the same. I was always well stocked up on blank tapes because I pinched so many.

CHRIS

I used to take the safety bit off the tape so no one could record over it. Then I'd get bored of those songs and put a bit of Sellotape over the holes and re-record over it. Things were so much more innocent in the eighties. One of our favourite games involved us going up to the phone box and dialling random numbers and making prank calls. And we used to do 'knock and run', which involved us knocking on people's doors and running away. Why?

STEPHEN

Kids don't move around so much now so they're all getting bigger. And someone told me the other day that the little shits are getting takeaways delivered to school at lunchtime.

CHRIS

I saw this poor kid the other day and she was so overweight she couldn't get across the road fast enough and she nearly got run over.

STEPHEN

People are arrogant about crossing the road now generally. They'll walk out in front of you while you're driving and eyeball you as if to say, 'Come on then! Run me over and see what fucking happens!' There's no Green Cross Code anymore. That man used to be terrifying.

Kids are too busy sitting in their rooms hacking into banks to have fun these days. Whenever you hear some big company has been hacked it always seems to have been some spotty little teenager in his bedroom.

CHRIS

Think what teenage boys could do if they used that intelligence for good.

To be fair, if we'd had mobile phones and the internet when I was a kid I would have been just as bad as kids are now. And I would probably be sat here with a full head of hair and double-D tits.

STEPHEN

Er, maybe we should get on to that later! I'll never forget this time when this man knocked on the back door asking for my mum. She'd popped out to get some shopping but I knew she was due back any minute so I ran to the front door and saw her walking down the road. She waved at me and I shouted at the top of my lungs, 'Muuuuum! The debt collector's here!' She was so furious.

CHRIS

I think because we were broke we used to make up games and stuff. We didn't have Xboxes and iPads so we used to play out on the street because we didn't have loads of toys. We had to make fun from nothing.

STEPHEN

We used to make our own water park, which basically involved getting in the bath and sliding up and down on a bar of soap. We'd do it for hours. I think when you're brought up on a budget and your mum can't afford to take you anywhere, things like walks down the park became an adventure. My mum was really good at turning simple things into an event. Even going to allotment was something we'd look forward to. Especially when it got dark and we used to nick everyone's vegetables.

I know that's a terrible thing to do but we had to do stuff like that to survive. We were dirt poor but looking back it was really character-building. Everyone pulled together and we'd have a lovely time doing things that cost nothing.

CHRIS

We weren't at all well off at all and we didn't get our first colour TV until I was eight. It was a hand-me-down from one of my dad's friends and it became our most prized possession.

STEPHEN

We rented our TV from Radio Rentals and it had a big box on the back you had to put 50p in to get it working. That would give you four hours' viewing. We'd put 50p in every night and at the end of the month Mr Radio Rentals would come and empty the box. He'd take out our rental money and enough to cover the TV licence and whatever was left over was given back to my mum. It was like a piggy bank for her. She knew that was coming at the end of every month so it was a bit of a bonus.

We used to be allowed to stay up late on a Wednesday because *Dallas* was on. We were supposed to go to bed at 8pm but as a treat we'd stay up until 9pm. Only if we had 50p to put in the box though. Sometimes we didn't have enough money to top it up and the TV would click off ten minutes before the end of a programme. And *Dallas* was all about the cliffhanger, wasn't it? Imagine the TV going dead just as they were about to reveal who shot JR?

If the TV did go off before the end of a show mum would let us stay up anyway, and she'd entertain us by taking her teeth out and gurning. Mum was only in her early thirties but she had all of her teeth out when she was 16 – probably because she ate too many sweets or something – so she was an expert gurner.

It's mad because I remember feeling so young when I was 32, and when I look back and think that my mum had five kids at that age it's shocking.

She couldn't work full-time because she had to look after us but she used to go out apple picking and cleaning and just about anything she could to get some money in. As soon as us kids were old enough we'd go out fruit picking with her in the summer holidays, and when we got a bit older we all got Saturday jobs and stuff.

CHRIS

Your mum had to do a lot because your dad wasn't around. My dad *was* around but he was either working or going fishing. Growing up it was always my mum, my two sisters and me hanging out together, so I had a lot of female influences in my early years. I think that's why I communicate so well with women now. And I hate it when men leave the toilet seat up!

STEPHEN

All the women in my life have been strong characters and the men have taken a bit of a back seat. I can't think of one positive male role model I had in my life. All my role models have been women like my mum, my nan, my aunties and my sisters. They're all strong and rule the roost.

CHRIS

My mum is like an ox. She raised all of us kids and she always found ways to make money. She didn't put up with any shit either. I remember her chasing women up the high street because they looked at her in a funny way.

She thought it was really funny to embarrass us kids whenever she could as well. She's got a bit of a dark side. She loved second-hand shops and back then they weren't in any way cool. Marie and I would be waiting at the bus stop after school and my mum would run out of the Oxfam opposite bellowing 'Coo-ey!' in front of our mates. She always timed it perfectly.

STEPHEN

I think I was more embarrassing to my mum than she was to me. I'll never forget when I was about seven or eight and I heard some music coming from the vicarage at the top of our estate. I went and had a look through the bushes and saw that there was a kids' fancy dress party going on. All these kids were dressed up as clowns and cowboys having a great time. But more importantly, there was a great big table of food.

CHRIS

He's got a real thing about food, this one.

STEPHEN

I could see all these amazing sweets and cakes so I went running home to my mum and said, 'The vicar's having a fancy dress party. Can I go?' We didn't have any fancy dress outfits I wanted to wear so she put me in a basque, stockings and stilettoes. Then she added a bit of make-up and shoved me out the door.

I walked into the vicarage and all these kids turned round and looked at me. I made a beeline for the food but before I could reach the table the vicar stopped me. He bent down and said to me, 'And who have you come as?' I looked up at him and replied, 'Me sister.'

I could walk straight down the hill to our house from the vicarage but when the party finished I decided I liked the way my outfit felt, so I took the long way round. I was walking down the road going 'clippety clop' and when I walked past the park I saw my brother and all his friends standing there looking really shocked. One of his mates shouted out, 'Oi, Paul, that's your brother!' Then someone shouted, 'Poof.'

That was the first time I'd ever heard that word, but it definitely wasn't the last. From then on people called me a poof regularly and it became almost like the norm. There was a gay guy who lived on the estate who was known as 'Poofy Dave', so people also started calling me Dave. I was a boy of many names.

CHRIS

I would have been so jealous of your outfit back then because I always wanted my own pair of heels. I used to get empty drink cans and squash them onto the bottoms of my shoes. I'd walk around really proudly in them because they made a similar sound to stilettoes. Then all my dreams came true.

When Marie was 12 and I was ten she bought a pair of electric-blue stilettoes and I was obsessed with them. Whenever she was out I'd nick them and wear them around the house. Marie would get home from school and scream, 'Mum, Chris has got my bloody shoes on again.'

We had a massive row about them once because I flatly refused to take them off and I said to her, 'You're just jealous because I walk in them better than you do.' It was true.

STEPHEN

I remember once Jill from next door was chucking out these high-heeled leather lace-up boots and Sharon begged my mum to be able to keep them. Mum agreed because she thought they'd be going in the dressing-up box, but the following Monday morning my sister came downstairs ready for school wearing them. She was only about seven and even though I wasn't much older I knew that was wrong. I said to my mum, 'You can't let her go to school in them. Look at the state of her.' My mum just shook her head and said, 'Fuck it, let her do it.' Next thing you know, Sharon is walking up the road to school like a bricklayer on stilts. That was one of my earliest moments of shame.

CHRIS

I used to argue with my sisters sometimes but we got on pretty well generally. Although I used to try and scare Sharon all the time. One time I was messing around with a lamp and the top came off so there was a live wire hanging out of the base. I told Sharon to touch it and she went, 'No, because I'm going to get hurt.' I told her I'd touched it and it was fine so she reached out her finger to it and she got electrocuted. She was so flustered she stepped back on to a balloon and burst it. My mum heard the commotion and shouted up the stairs asking what was going on. I lied and said Sharon had got scared because I knew I'd get into so much trouble if my mum thought I'd electrocuted my sister.

Another time she was on her bed listening to her Walkman and she was so into it she had her eyes closed. I crept up the stairs and squeezed my face in between the bannisters and waited until she opened her eyes. When she eventually saw me she screamed so much she hit her head on the wall. I was so mean.

STEPHEN

You do pick on each when you're kids though, don't you? And you also run to your mum and grass each other up. But if our mum was ever pissed off with us we'd club together and put on a united front.

My sister Sharon once tried to make custard and she ruined the kitchen. There was powder and milk *everywhere*. When mum got back she asked who'd made the mess and said she was going to give us all a hiding unless someone admitted it was their fault. We all knew it was Sharon but we wanted to protect her so Denise, Paul and I all got smacked bottoms. When it was Sharon's turn to get a smack she blurted out, 'It was me!' so she bloody got away with it.

CHRIS

One of my favourite things to do when I was a kid was make mud pies. I'd create a pop-up café in the back garden and try and sell them to friends and family, and my mum would always pretend to eat them and tell me how delicious they were. I loved making camps too.

STEPHEN

Me too. We'd get all the sheets and towels out and drape them over the furniture.

CHRIS

Marie and I had bunk beds when we were in the cemetery lodge and every morning we used to get a bed sheet and stuff it underneath the top mattress so it hung down and covered the bottom bunk. We'd play in there for hours. My mum used to get so annoyed but I always blamed Sharon, even though she was so small she was still in a cot. I got away with everything when I was a kid because I was the middle child and the only boy.

I put the fact that I'm a fussy eater down to my childhood. Because I was the favourite my mum used to pander to me, whereas my sisters had to eat whatever they were given. Even to this day it's a real problem and I'm very picky.

STEPHEN

I was such a wimp when I was younger. I'd cry at the drop of a hat. When my first rabbit, Noir, died (I inherited that name and didn't have a clue what it meant but I thought it was exotic because it was foreign) I sat at the windowsill for three days sobbing and looking out into the garden. On day three my mum said, 'Oh, fucking leave off will you?' and I had to pretend I was okay.

A while later someone gave me two more rabbits, and because they were show rabbits they had little silver rings around their legs. They were beautiful. I kept them in the shed and I was as pleased as punch with them.

When my cousin Tony came round to visit a few days later I took him out to the shed to show them to him. It was in the middle of winter and when Tony looked in the hutch he said, 'They're fucking dead!' They'd frozen to death and they were completely solid. I was devastated and I felt so bad. I can't remember what they were called.

We got one more rabbit after that, because my mate Sarah-Jane decided she didn't want hers anymore and gave it to Beverley. It was massive and looked more like a hare, and when my mum went out to hang out some washing one day it reared up at her and bared its teeth. She ran back into the house and said, 'Fucking get rid of *that*.' And that was the end of him.

After that we decided to scrap rabbits, and on my tenth birthday I got Charlie, a little Jack Russell. He was my best friend for ten years. We used to let him roam around the streets on his own but we always knew where to find him. He used to go to this old lady's house to have a bacon sandwich for breakfast every day. Then he'd go to someone else's house for a bit of lunch. Then at about 3pm he knew the kids were coming out of school so he'd go and hang outside the shop nearby and wait for them to give him sweets.

CHRIS

You can tell he was your dog because he was always trying to get food off people.

STEPHEN

He was so clever. People claimed they'd seen him on buses going to the next village or waiting at traffic lights for them to change. He honestly thought he was human.

To get to my school you had to leave the estate and walk across a really busy main road. He'd walk us kids up to the main road and then we'd say, 'Home now, Charlie,' so he'd turn around and run back to the house. Sometimes I'd come out of school and he'd be there waiting for me. God knows how he knew what time it was.

We were so close and I thought the world of him, but when I was 20 the local dogcatcher caught him for about the seventh time. I wasn't working at the time and it was going to cost £31.50 to get him out. I was desperately trying to raise the money, which was a lot back then, but by the time I got it and went to collect him they'd put him down. I still dream about Charlie all the time and think about how much I let him down.

CHRIS

That's so awful. They knew where you lived and they still did that. What bastards.

I had quite a few pets growing up. We had three gerbils called Mick, Mick-Mick and Mickey. Then Mick died so we only had Mick-Mick and Mickey, and I hated Mickey. He once latched onto my finger and bit it really hard and after that I wouldn't go near him. We had a sheepdog called Blackie too.

After Blackie died when I was about seven we got Winnie, who was a Jack Russell cross. She was a lovely dog and, like Charlie, she liked going out to roam on her own. One day we realized she was pregnant so it's quite clear what she was getting up to on her trips out.

She had four puppies and we kept the two boys, Sparky and Prince, and found homes for the two girls. They were all mongrels and Sparky looked like a Dobermann, while Prince was like a scruffy Border terrier.

I adored Sparky but he and Prince used to fight all the time so we had no choice but to get rid of one. We couldn't decide which one to let go of so in the end we thought it was kinder to give them both away. A week later poor Winnie ran out into the road and got killed, so we were left without any dogs at all. We were all so upset.

We didn't have any pets for a few years and then, on her fifteenth birthday, Marie insisted she wanted a cat, so she got a white fluffy thing called Tara. And of course because she had a cat Sharon and I wanted one.

We ended up with Tuppence and Buttons, and then Tara got pregnant and had four kittens. Because Marie was a goth she called them Sevi, after Steven Severin from Siouxsie and the Banshees, Nephi, after the band Fields of the Nephilim, and then Sisi and Ciro, who got off lightly.

About a year later we ended up with another two cats, Pepe, after Pepe Le Pew, and Tammy. My mum turned into a bit of a mad cat lady. She had eight cats at one point, which is a bit excessive.

We've gone off on an animal tangent. Let's talk about school. My schooldays were *horrific*.

STEPHEN

I started nursery school with a broken leg. I'm not sure if that was because of that fall in my house or whether it was a result of the time Paul convinced me to put my leg out in front of a car.

CHRIS

I'm surprised you managed to survive your childhood.

STEPHEN

I know. I remember this time when Paul dropped a paving

slab on Denise's foot. When my mum took her sock off her big toe was hanging off, and now her toenail is so thick she has to cut it with a knife.

I was quite accident-prone as a kid. When I was really young I fell over a safety gate and had to have five stitches in my tongue. Then, a few weeks later, I fell over the same safety gate and cracked my head open. So I suppose it wasn't that much of a surprise when I started nursery in plaster.

This girl called Mandy had to look after me and help me get around because of my leg and I was really cross because she stank of piss. I did like nursery though. I liked getting a bottle of milk every lunchtime.

CHRIS

Yeah, until Margaret Thatcher stopped it all. One of my earliest memories is of being at playschool and one of the teachers saying to us, 'You won't have milk anymore because Margaret Thatcher's taken it away.' I also remember being given this little book about Lady Di and Charles' wedding. I couldn't read it but I enjoyed looking at pictures of Di's swishy hair.

STEPHEN

Aww, Lady Di. I was such a fan. Everyone remembers where they were when she died don't they? I was in some club in Vauxhall and I came out hammered and some Italian bloke said to me, 'Your Princess, she is *dead*.' I was like, 'Whaaaaaat?' When I got to the train station and saw it on the front page I was so shocked and upset.

CHRIS

I remember being in my rented house in Bois Moor Road in Chesham the Sunday it happened. I turned the TV on and they kept referring to 'the Princess's friends and family'. I sat there for about half an hour watching it and then it suddenly clicked. Paul, my partner at the time, walked in and I said to him, 'I think Princess Diana's dead.'

STEPHEN

In a totally unrelated incident I once woke up on a mate's sofa with a *really* bad hangover. I turned on the telly and the newsreader said something like, 'Right, we're going live to London now. The spacecraft is still visible but no one's made any contact yet.' Then they cut to this scene of London with a spaceship hovering above Buckingham Palace. I was like, 'What the *fuck*?' Then I realized I was watching a film.

CHRIS

You idiot.

STEPHEN

I do find the conspiracy theories about Princess Diana interesting, but I don't think we actually live in that sort of world, do we? People don't really bump other people off, do they?

CHRIS

It's such a touchy subject isn't it? I'm a real royalist so I refuse to believe anything bad about them. And of course I fancy Prince Harry. He's the one you'd want to go out with, isn't he? Doesn't he look gorgeous with a beard? I love gingers. I've started to like gingers more and more as I've got older. I used to like William too but I went off him when his hair started thinning. Not that I'm shallow or anything.

STEPHEN

Prince William looks like a *Spitting Image* puppet now. Andrew was good looking back in the day but now he's a fat lump. I like Harry too though. He's lovely. And gingers have massive willies.

CHRIS

That's true. This guy I was at secondary school with had really vivid ginger hair and he wasn't at all good looking but all the girls loved him. Maybe that was why?

I was so shy when I first went to playschool. I remember so clearly having my photo taken and I was so nervous that I wouldn't look at the photographer. The teacher told me to look at my mum instead. I was only about three. You can see it in the picture section. It's the one where I look really angelic.

Even then I didn't like being away from my family. I've got great memories of growing up at home but very few of being at school. I stuck out and I was different, because I wasn't your typical lad, so I was bullied from the age of seven until I was 19.

Some of the bullies that picked on me used to hang out with my sisters. So even when I was at home where I felt safest, sometimes they would be there taking the piss out of me. They'd be nice to me in front of my family, but as soon as their backs were turned they'd be poking fun at me and calling me names.

There were times when I didn't even feel comfortable in my own house and I felt like I had nowhere to escape to. The people who lived next door also used to get their young kids to scream abuse up at my bedroom window. The parents would be stood there laughing. I never understood why I got picked on so badly.

As I got older, Sharon used to protect me if someone had a go at me. Some bloke in a pub called me 'queer' once and she had him outside in a headlock, punching him in the face. She was the most butch out of the three of us.

STEPHEN

I remember when my mum sent us to do judo when I was a kid and I was up against this really short girl. I walked into the ring with her and she picked me up and threw me straight on the floor. She started trying to bully me at school after that because she clearly saw me as an easy target. But my sister Denise wasn't having any of it and she warned her off by throwing her down a staircase. She got two weeks in exclusion for that.

Mum tried to get us to go back to judo the following week and Paul was really up for it but I was having none of it.

CHRIS

It's funny that both of our sisters stood up for us. The bullying got to me so badly at times.

STEPHEN

We did reclaim your childhood nickname a few years ago though.

CHRIS

We did. I was called 'Chrissy Sissy' from a really young age so Stephen had a mug made with it written on the front in big letters. So the nickname became mine in a way, and it started bothering me less. Of course people don't call me that anymore but I think I'd been carrying it with me and it still hurt. Now I don't feel as scared of it anymore. I don't love it but I feel a bit indifferent to it.

Since I've been on *Gogglebox* some of the people who bullied me have got in touch on Facebook wanting to be friends. A few of them have even apologized to me. One of my sister's old mates said to her recently, 'I'd love to see your brother again. I really admired him growing up for just being who he was.' Seriously, why would I want to see him? He was so vile to me back then.

STEPHEN

I always felt like I stood out at school too. Because I was suddenly around a lot of other kids I started noticing things I hadn't been aware of before, like cool trainers and nice watches. And I knew my mum would never be able to afford to buy me those things.

I was really lucky I didn't get bullied too badly though. I think a lot of that was down the fact I had an older brother. Also, even though I was a little gay boy, I could still handle myself. If someone started on me I'd bite back and I think my mouth put the bullies off. I used to get called gypsy and pikey a lot but I used to answer back and people rarely challenged me. I didn't have that many loyal friends though. I think people were scared to be my mate in case they got bullied as a result.

CHRIS

You became the joker of the class to make things easier on yourself, didn't you?

STEPHEN

I did. I took the piss out of myself before anyone else got a chance, and the things they said about me were never as bad as the things I said about myself.

CHRIS

I was too scared to do that. Plus I had no one sticking up for me. Kids used to call me names and kick balls at me in the playground. It hugely affected me growing up and because of the bullying I never felt good enough. I still don't, sometimes.

STEPHEN

It takes a long time to shake that feeling off.

CHRIS

It does, but I do think it's part of the reason a lot of gay men become very successful – because they want to prove to themselves and other people that they're worthy and good enough.

STEPHEN

Like Chris, when Facebook first started I got lots of friend requests from people I knew at school. I was travelling at the time and I was at Base Camp One at Mount Everest and loads of people sent me messages saying, 'You look like you've done so much with your life.' Then I looked through their profile pages and a lot of them are still back in my home town, looking haggard and miserable. Some of them have got six kids by three different women or they've just got out of prison. So really, I'm glad I went through those few years of being picked on, because my life has turned out so much better than theirs. Being bullied makes you quite defiant and turns you into a bit of a fighter.

CHRIS

One of the worst things that happened to me bullying-wise was when I was 17 and I got invited to this guy Julian's eighteenth birthday party by some local boys. I didn't really know Julian but I was so excited because I felt like I was finally being accepted.

From that night onwards, I got on really well with Julian and we went on to become best friends. A few months later he turned round to me and said, 'I've got something I need to tell you. You were brought to my party by that group of lads because they wanted me to smack your face in.' It turned out that his birthday present from these lads was the chance to kick the shit out of me. Nice, eh?

But I got my revenge. Bruce, the guy who had set me up to get beaten up, started trying to be matey with me after that. We were all going to a party so I offered to buy him some cider to take. I took it back to mine, drank some with Julian, weed in it and did the bottle back up. We got to the party and he downed it because he never shared his drinks with anyone. As soon as he'd finished the last mouthful I said to him, 'Did you enjoy your drink? Are you *pissed* yet?' To this day he still doesn't know he got pissed on my piss.

Chapter Two

SANTA'S COMING

Chris: 'Do you remember when I bought you an Advent calendar and you ate the lot on 1 December?'
Stephen: 'I do. You said to me, "You can't do that!" and I replied, "Course I can. They're my fucking chocolates".'

CHRIS

I think growing up you feel like you want to be mates with everyone and be really popular. Then you get to a certain point in your life where that becomes really tiring and you just want good friends around you. You end up sacking off the waste-of-space people and just keeping the good ones.

When you're younger you want quantity rather than quality and I was desperate to be liked by the entire school.

But you streamline as you get older and you end up with a small but perfectly formed little group. Stephen's got some amazing friends but he can count them on one hand.

STEPHEN

I've got five really close friends, Kerry, Lorna, Melissa, Malden and Lee.

CHRIS

Erm, what about me? Don't I make it onto your first hand? I'll settle for being number six then. Thanks for that.

STEPHEN

They don't hang out with each other and their paths don't often cross. They only meet up if they're at one of my birthday dos or something.

I hardly speak to them from one month to the next but when I do there's no, 'I haven't heard from you for ages'. We just catch up and have a laugh.

I'm always myself with my mates but I know how far I can push it with each one. I can be ruder with some and take the piss out of other ones more.

I like just meeting up with one person when I go out so we can have a proper conversation. I hate big groups and I really like my own company. I would rather be on my own than at a big party full of people.

SANTA'S COMING

CHRIS

I like my own company too. I'm quite happy pottering around at home on my own. I'm not someone who needs to be around other people all the time.

STEPHEN

I've never had a big group of gay friends because, from experience, they all get off with each other and it becomes bitchy. I can't be bothered with talking behind other people's backs and all that shit. If I've got something to say about someone, I'll say it to them.

CHRIS

The thing is, with real friends they can really piss you off at times but you just let it go. Stephen pisses me off *all* the time but I just get on with it. That's when you know someone is a real friend.

STEPHEN

None of my friends I have now are from school. I dropped them like a hot brick as soon as I could.

CHRIS

I'm still in contact with a few people from school. I felt a bit down the other day because someone put our fifth-year photo on Facebook. I got tagged and everyone was commenting on it and I spotted Ollie, who was my first crush.

I thought he was so gorgeous and we became best friends for a while. I felt like there was something between us but he was straight. I even tried to set him up with my sister, Sharon. I really wanted to be with him, but I had to make do with spending time with him instead.

The awful thing is, he stole one of my dad's rings that I'd inherited and I was so angry I completely cut him off. A few years later I found out from his ex-girlfriend that he was into dressing in women's clothes and that he was in love with me. Tragically he died a few years ago and it makes me feel so sad that we never knew each other felt that way.

That Facebook photo took me right back to those days and I felt all those emotions I did when I was a teenager again. I was different; I was the odd one out. People didn't seem to want to be friends with me. . . And throughout it all there was this guy who was going through the same thing as me and we could have been there for each other. I think that's such a shame.

STEPHEN
That is really sad. That poor guy.

CHRIS
I know, Widdle.

STEPHEN

It's funny when you call me Widdle. Do you remember how everyone had nicknames when you were young?

My nickname has always been Widdle because when I was really little I went to the loo for a wee on my own and I put my willy back into my pants without shaking it. When I pulled up my trousers I had widdle marks on them and when I walked into the living room my Uncle Cyril said, 'Oh, look at Widdle!' It's stuck to this day.

My sister was Dirty Knick, Paul was Webby, because of our surname, Sharon was Shaz (simple but effective) and Beverley was Pixie, because she looked like a little pixie when she was a baby.

CHRIS

When my sister Sharon was 11 and her mate Tracey was 12 they used to hang out with older boys and drive around the estate, and all the lads gave them the nicknames 11 and 12.

I know this bloke everyone called Wonky Eyed Joe. Funnily enough, it was because he had a wonky eye. He had an operation to fix it but it didn't work so now he's called Still Wonky Eyed Joe.

Do you think people ever know they have nicknames? You get so many people called something like 'Fat Sue' or 'Grumpy Bob', but do they actually know people call them that?

STEPHEN

I was sometimes called Little Stephen and my cousin, Stephen, was known as Big Stephen. Even now we call him that.

Someone called me Little Stephen the other day and I felt about ten again. It's weird how feelings come rushing back to you so easily.

When I go to a council estate now I get the same feelings I had when I lived on one. I've got nothing against council estates whatsoever but they do bring up strange memories for me.

CHRIS

When my mum had a hip replacement a couple of years ago I went and stayed at her flat in Chesham to look after her cat. She's got loads of pictures on the walls of me and my sisters when we were kids and I had the worst night's sleep ever. I woke up hyperventilating because I felt like I was that unhappy young boy again.

STEPHEN

My mum moved out of Sittingbourne years ago thankfully, and wherever I've moved to she's ended up in the same place. Now she's in a position where I make sure she's comfortable and doesn't want for anything. She worked bloody hard for all those years to bring all of us kids up so she deserves to be taken care of.

She may get bored of living in our little village sometimes, but she's more content than I've ever seen her. For her to go from never having anything to knowing she's got no financial worries is so nice.

CHRIS

You can tell she really appreciates it and she feels settled. The highlight of her week is going to Iceland, isn't it?

STEPHEN

It is. She loves it.

CHRIS

When we were dating each other we turned into our mums. I remember us going to a McDonalds drive-through and I was getting the order wrong like my mum would, and you were moaning at me like *your* mum would.

My mum always says things wrong. She'll call me the name of everyone else in my family before she gets mine right. She always refers to stuff as a 'thingy' and you have to guess what she's on about. The thing is now my fiancé Tony and I do exactly the same. We can have an entire conversation about 'thingies' and know what each other is talking about. It's like a sixth sense.

STEPHEN

I do think I'm becoming more and more like my mum, and I do feel old sometimes. I was cutting this lady's hair in the salon the other day. She was probably about 60 and we were chatting away and it suddenly dawned on me that I've got more in common with her than I have with a 25-year-old. I'll be 50 in five years' time. How?

CHRIS

Two of my best friends, Julia and Sarah, are in their early sixties, but they don't seem like they are. Sarah and I have chicks and dicks night – which is actually chips and dips – and we have such a laugh. Her eldest son is the same age as me so I'm basically hanging out with someone's mum. It's mad, but I just don't notice the age difference at all.

STEPHEN

For me, the height of friendship rudeness is someone turning up at my house unannounced.

CHRIS

What, like you do to me? *All* the time?

STEPHEN

I suppose I do actually. I also hate it if someone phones you in the evening. I would never consider ringing a landline after 9pm. And I always screen my calls on my mobile. I often tell people I'm filming even when I'm not if I don't want to answer the phone.

SANTA'S COMING

CHRIS

I hope you don't do that to me? The only time I ignore calls is when I'm really busy with work or if it's a special day, like my birthday or Christmas, and I just want to relax.

STEPHEN

Birthdays should be the one day you can do whatever you want. You don't want to be answering the phone to someone wishing you happy birthday every five minutes. Send a text! Christmas should be a day of rest too.

Christmas was so brilliant in our house when I was growing up. We all picked the place where we wanted to open our presents so we all knew where to sit when we went into the living room in the morning.

We'd charge down first thing and wait for mum to get up and then we'd get stuck in. My mum used to get herself in debt with the Provident every year so she could buy us nice presents, and then she'd spend the rest of the year paying it off.

CHRIS

My mum did the same. One of my earliest memories of Christmas is going off to bed feeling really excited because I knew Santa was going to come and fill my sack. But when I woke up there weren't any presents and I was so upset. I fell back to sleep and when I woke up again Santa had finally been and I was so happy.

STEPHEN

We were allowed to open one present on Christmas Eve before we went to bed, and it was always gutting if you chose a shit one.

CHRIS

We didn't get loads of presents. It was usually things like colouring books and jigsaws, but they were always very thoughtful.

STEPHEN

Christmas was all about the food for us. Mum used to put everything on display along the sideboard in the living room and all the food was completely symmetrical. If there was a pineapple up one end there would also be one up the other. And we always had a big wicker basket filled with fruit in the middle. It was all laid out so perfectly. For one day we felt like we had everything.

Everyone in my family went to my nan's house on Boxing Day. That was the best part of Christmas for us kids because we'd get to see all our aunts and uncles and cousins. Christmas Day was a lot of fun but Boxing Day was what we all looked forward to. There would be a full spread of vol-au-vents, crisps and sausage rolls, and we'd all eat until we were stuffed.

There were tons of us and we'd all squeeze into her three-bedroomed house and party from 2pm until around midnight.

Most of my family are ex-Londoners so they loved a good cockney knees up. We'd sing songs like 'Roll Out the Barrel' and 'Maybe It's Because I'm a Londoner'. We'd play charades and we'd all get up and sing for everyone. My song was usually 'Down at the Old Bull and Bush'.

We did that every year without fail, but when my nan died that all kind of fell apart.

CHRIS

Stephen's whole family love Chaz and Dave.

STEPHEN

We do. We had a Chaz and Dave tribute act at my fortieth birthday party and at my sister Beverley's wedding.

I remember dancing with my aunties and because some of their clothes were made from nylon they'd make crackling noises. I'd hear a sound like two sticks being rubbed together and know it was their tights.

My aunties always bought us the same presents every year. My auntie Bid would buy us pyjamas, my auntie Joan would buy us slippers and my auntie Sylvie would buy us socks and vests. It was always stuff we needed to help my mum out.

CHRIS

When I was about 13 I started decorating the house for my mum. She wasn't very good at it and she used to cover the ceiling with those really cheap paperchain decorations. So I took charge and made it look so much better, even if I do say so myself.

STEPHEN

We always had paper chains on the ceiling too. We made our own and we'd hang balloons in between.

CHRIS

I refused to put up the paperchains and I got my mum to buy tinsel decorations instead. It looked like an Indian take-away. I covered the ceiling in so much sparkly stuff I was worried it was going to fall down.

A couple of years later I started going into the countryside with Sharon and cutting holly, ivy and foliage, and we'd make amazing arrangements. I used to get black electrical tape and criss-cross it on our windows so it looked like they were made from leaded glass. I'd add snow spray to the corners and it would take my mum until the next Christmas to get rid of it all.

One year we didn't have much money so we couldn't afford a Christmas tree. Sharon and I went out looking for one in the woods near our house but we couldn't find anything that would work. In the end I went and cut down a conifer that was in one of our neighbours' front gardens. I waited until it was dark and then I hacked it down with one of my dad's old saws. It wasn't the prettiest tree we've ever had.

SANTA'S COMING

I always loved decorating the Christmas tree. A lot of my friends have got kids and I love seeing their trees. They're always really sparse at the top and full of decorations down the bottom because that's the only place they can reach.

These days my Christmas trees always look like an OTT drag queen. They have to be all-singing and all-dancing. My friends always say you can tell it's a gay man's tree.

STEPHEN

All fur coat and no knickers? Mum used to hang chocolates on our tree and we'd unwrap them really carefully, take the chocolate out and then re-wrap them into the same shape. These empty bits of tin foil would be blowing in the wind but she never cottoned on.

CHRIS

Do you remember when I bought you an Advent calendar and you ate the lot on 1 December?

STEPHEN

I do. You said to me, 'You can't do that!' and I replied, 'Course I can. They're my fucking chocolates.'

It was always so depressing when all the Christmas decorations came down in January. All the rooms looked so bare and empty it was like you'd been robbed.

CHRIS

And there was always an echo in the house.

STEPHEN

And you could see the brown woodchip on the walls again.

CHRIS

My dad knew this old man who didn't have any family so he used to come round to ours every Christmas. He just used to sit in the corner quietly and he always brought us sweets. Then one year he didn't bring us any sweets and my mum didn't let him come back again.

The highlight of mine and my sisters' Christmas was always *Top of the Pops*. We looked forward to that all day. Christmas TV used to be so good back then but it's awful now. *The Sound of Music* is *always* on. You'd think they could find some new films.

STEPHEN

Gone with the Wind, a Bond film and *The Wizard of* Oz will be on at some point without fail. I could watch *Gone with the Wind* over and over again though. Four Christmases ago it was on at 9am on Christmas Day and my mum and I got up early specially to watch it and it was so lovely. It's bloody long though.

I love Christmas songs but some of them make me feel

a bit melancholy. Maria Carey's 'All I Want For Christmas Is You' is a classic though.

CHRIS

I love 'Rockin' Around the Christmas Tree', the Kim Wilde version. There's a brilliant video of her singing it on the Underground a few years ago. She got everyone singing and it was lovely.

STEPHEN

The problem with Christmas now is that it starts so early. The older I get the more I think it should be changed so we just have it every two years. That way it would feel a little bit more special. It comes round so quickly.

There are lots of things I like about it. It's definitely a time when you think of others. Even if they don't appreciate it.

CHRIS

I said to Tony last year that we should see if there are any old people down our road that are going to be alone. Even if we just pop in and see them for ten minutes and take them a box of chocolates or invite them round to ours, it could make all the difference.

One of the best Christmases I ever had was when I went out partying on Christmas Eve until 4.30am. I'd pulled this bloke in a bar and we were walking down St James's Street in Brighton and he was trying to be all romantic so he picked me up and tried to throw me against this lamp post so he could snog me. But he was so drunk he missed and basically chucked me into the road and then fell on top of me.

I was so hungover and bruised the next day I grabbed my duvet and lay on the sofa until about 3pm. Then I made myself a little Christmas dinner, got ready and went to a house party. Loved it.

STEPHEN

Christmas is a nice excuse to get everyone together and see your family, but it is a lot of pressure.

CHRIS

So many people get stressed and have breakdowns over one day. It makes me laugh when people go Christmas shopping on Christmas Eve and they're grabbing everything in sight like the shops are closing forever.

Stephen and I went shopping on Christmas Eve when we were together and people were pushing each other out of the way and snatching things off shelves. Their massive trolleys were overflowing with stuff they probably didn't end up eating. I looked at Stephen and said, 'What are they doing? The shops open again on Boxing Day.'

STEPHEN

I remember that day. We got a turkey crown, a couple of

carrots, Brussel sprouts and some potatoes and we were sorted. That's all we needed.

CHRIS

We used to love going shopping together, didn't we? The first thing we always used to do is go to the fruit and veg aisle and pick out a carrot each.

Stephen would always pick a small one and I'd pick out a big one. It was like a little ritual. There was no talking involved and we'd both hold up a different carrot and we'd nod or shake our heads depending on whether we liked them or not.

When we got to the checkout the cashier would pick up these two carrots – one really tiny and one really massive – and give us such a look. We'd act like it was the most normal thing in the world.

Christmas these days means a break for me. Every year work is really, really busy in the run up because everyone wants their hair done so they look nice in the Christmas photos.

I usually end up exhausted by Christmas Eve but this year I've booked myself off for the entire Christmas period. I can't wait. Christmas week is *all* about me.

STEPHEN

I'll have to work because it will be one of our busiest times in the salon. But I will do absolutely fuck all for several days.

It'll just be mum and I this year because my other half, Daniel, is going to see his parents, and I know we'll just eat and eat. Unless I'm on a health kick, in which case my Christmas dinner will comprise of lettuce and dust.

I don't drink that much over Christmas anymore. I used to drink loads when I was younger and it was a brilliant excuse for a knees up. But my mum doesn't usually drink indoors, so she might have a Pernod or two but neither of us will be going crazy.

CHRIS

My auntie Helen was the first person who gave me booze, and that was one Christmas when I was about 11. She wasn't my real auntie. She was an auntie in the same way everyone is when you're a kid.

She always had a bottle of Woodpecker cider at her house and I was allowed a tiny glass when we went to visit on Christmas Eve. After that it became a bit of a tradition and when I got into my teens my mum would buy me a big bottle and I had to make it last all Christmas and New Year.

STEPHEN

I remember going up to the shop and getting my mum 20 fags one Christmas when I was about seven. No one cared back then. They'd serve kids.

CHRIS

But then when you were actually old enough to buy cigarettes they would ask you for ID.

STEPHEN

I got IDed when I was buying booze recently. I said to the bloke serving me, 'Are you taking the piss?' and he said yes and laughed. My heart did flutter momentarily.

CHRIS

Were you thinking that your fillers and Botox were worth every penny?

I remember Sharon getting drunk at a wedding when she was about eight. She was going up the bar and pretending to get Babysham for my mum and they gave it to her!

She was drunk on the dance floor and she nearly fell onto the wedding cake. My mum had popped out to see someone so my dad was supposed to be looking after us, and when she got back half an hour later Sharon was plastered. We didn't get invited to any more family weddings after that. I don't think kids should be invited to weddings anyway.

They're always rolling around the dance floor getting in the way.

I remember being given a stuffed donkey for Christmas when I was about five and I thought it was incredible. It was almost the same size as me and I thought it was the best thing ever.

My mum used to buy all our presents from a catalogue and I used to go through it with her helping her to choose things for Sharon and Marie. I used to say, 'Sharon would love that!' and point at all the things *I* wanted.

I used to hide them in the loft for my mum because I was the only one who could get up there. But I'd always sneak up and have a little play before Christmas. I'd open all the boxes and reseal them really carefully so no one could tell.

The best Christmas present I ever got was an R2-D2 when I was about eight and I've still got it now. Even though I wasn't really into boys' toys I thought it was *so* cool. A few years later I decided I was all grown up and I didn't want toys anymore, so I put a load into a box and asked my mum to get rid of them for me.

Mum gave them to her friend's son, David, but two days later I started crying because I missed my R2-D2. Luckily David's mum had kept it safe for me because she had a feeling I might want it back.

I loved cuddly toys as a kid and I had so many lined up on my bed there was hardly any room for me to sleep. I had my Donkey, Ding Dong Ted, Roly, and so on. They were all arranged in size order. Little Ted was always my favourite so I always cuddled him when I went to sleep.

STEPHEN

The only thing I kept from my childhood was a picture my sister Beverley drew me on her first day at infant school. It was a tree with two branches, a rabbit and a sun. When she had her baby shower a couple of years ago I had it framed and gave it back to her and she hung it in her son Jessie's room. It makes me feel all emotional.

CHRIS

You can be quite sweet sometimes.

STEPHEN

I was always playing with my sisters' dolls and prams when I was young and my mum said to me one Christmas, 'I know what I'm going to buy you for Christmas – a doll's pram.' Honestly, my eyes lit up. I didn't realize she was joking and I visualized exactly what it would look like.

It was going to be burgundy corduroy with some kind of satin trim and I was so disappointed when I didn't get it. I always really wanted a Girl's World as well. I used to play with my sisters' one for hours.

CHRIS

Do you remember the Barbie with the long hair you could pull out? Every girl I knew cut it all off so their Barbie ended up with a pineapple on top of her head. Why? Did they think it was going to magically grow again?

STEPHEN

I found out Father Christmas didn't exist thanks to my uncle Cyril. I was about five and he said to me, 'You're not getting any presents this year. Father Christmas couldn't handle it so he's hung himself.'

CHRIS

Nice.

STEPHEN

I told my mum expecting her to try and make it all better and she said, 'Nah, Cyril's right. He doesn't exist. Sorry.'

Christmas can be fun but I've never liked New Year. It's boring and it's always a let-down. You pay £30 to get into a pub that's usually free and then you queue for an hour to get a drink.

CHRIS

Why should you have to pay to get into a pub? You're going to spend loads of money on booze so they should be grateful to have you in there.

I had a really awful New Year in my late teens. Me and Maria, who was one of my best mates, went to a fancy dress party. She went as a belly dancer and I decided to go dressed as a slutty girl. I probably looked a bit like a prostitute, if I'm being honest.

It was such a boring party we decided to get the train to London to see the New Year in there. We got a taxi to Northwood Hills train station and Maria ran ahead of me down the steps onto the packed platform. I tried to keep up with her but the steps were really thin and I had these big wooden clogs on. I slipped on the first step and bumped all the way down to the bottom and fell in a heap in front of loads of people. One of my clogs snapped in half and all these guys ran over to me and said, 'Are you alright, love?' and helped me up. All I kept thinking was, 'I hope they don't clock that I'm a bloke.'

Maria convinced me we should still go to London and said that we could both wear half of the broken clog each. I have no idea why but it seemed like a great thing to do at the time.

I was in absolute agony trying to walk on the back section of a broken clog. Then by the time we got to London we'd missed midnight anyway. We'd also missed the last train home so we ended up spending the whole night walking around Soho. I'm sure some of the prostitutes thought we were touting for business.

For the last couple of years I've gone round to my friend

Julia's for New Year. Julia is like my Brighton mum and she's got such an eclectic group of friends from all walks of life. It's very relaxed and laid back and we all gather to toast the New Year and clink glasses at midnight. It's so much nicer than being in a crowded bar with a load of pissed people you don't know.

STEPHEN

I hate the countdown to the New Year. The clock strikes midnight and absolutely nothing changes. Then people play 'Auld Lang Syne' and that depresses the hell out of me.

TV shows do tributes to all the celebrities that have died that year, which isn't exactly uplifting. There's *always* someone on the list you didn't realize had died. It's going to be a bloody long list this year, isn't it?

CHRIS

God yes, what a terrible year. So many have gone. Prince, Victoria Wood and Caroline Aherne.

STEPHEN

Ronnie Corbett, Terry Wogan, Muhammad Ali, Alan Rickman. David Bowie, David Gest. Well, this is cheery.

Swiftly changing the subject, what were your birthdays like growing up? Mine weren't really a big deal. I didn't have my first birthday party until I was 33. I think because there were so many of us it would have cost a fortune for my mum to keep arranging celebrations.

CHRIS

I remember going to some birthday parties when I was a kid and I'd always go to the corner shop on the way and get a lucky bag or something as a present.

STEPHEN

I went to one girl's birthday party in McDonalds and I thought it was so sophisticated. It was the first time I ever had a McDonalds. But clearly not the last.

I loved that period of time from October onwards. You could earn so much money. You could do penny for the guy, trick or treat *and* sing Christmas carols. We'd do it all.

Me and Sharon were really inventive. When I was about 11 we got her cleanest teddy and took it door to door on the estate saying we were having a raffle. We gave everyone a ticket and then we decided who we wanted to win. We gave it to this old lady in the end and she was so chuffed.

CHRIS

I was the best at making costumes for all mine and my sisters' dolls growing up. I made Sindy this amazing devil outfit for Halloween. I also made her a wedding dress, inspired by Princess Diana's meringue.

59

One Halloween when I was about 12 I dressed up as Dracula, Sharon dressed up as a vampire bride and my friend Maria was a devil. We decided to go round all the local pubs trick or treating. We thought we'd rake it in but when we walked into the first pub I said, 'Trick or treat?' and some bloke turned round and said, 'Trick, or fuck off.' We stood there in silence for about five minutes and then we realized it was a lost cause and walked home.

STEPHEN

If people asked us for a trick they had to put their hand in this carrier bag we took round with us. We'd tell them it was full of flour, eggs and dog shit to make them give us a treat.

My friend Martin could throw up on demand, so sometimes if people asked us for a trick he'd do that for them. I don't think they were expecting that.

One year when we did penny for the Guy we couldn't be bothered to make a proper Guy so we put Beverley in a pram and stuck a blanket over her head. She was probably only about three and we pushed her door to door with her legs hanging out.

We were always finding new ways to make money. If we wanted sweets we'd make the money somehow. We used to knock on our neighbours' doors and ask people if they wanted any odd jobs done. We'd wash cars, mow lawns – you name it. I don't think kids do that these days do they?

CHRIS

I remember when Ouija boards became a real trend one Halloween. Most people used to write letters on a piece of paper and use a glass, but I went one stage further and I made a *proper* board. I swear it used to work.

STEPHEN

We used to use Ouija boards as well. We kind of knew someone was moving the glass but we still got really into it. One of the girls would usually end up crying or pretend she'd been possessed.

CHRIS

One evening, some friends and I were messing around with a Ouija board in my bedroom and the TV was on with the volume turned up. Then we realized there was no sound coming from it. We all turned and looked at it and the volume knob moved up on its own and the sound started again. Honestly. Cross my heart and hope to die, it happened.

STEPHEN

There were some weird trends around when we were growing up. Like wearing one luminous orange sock and one green one.

CHRIS

And shell suits.

STEPHEN

And yellow and blue roller skates. They were so cool. Playing Bulldog was a big thing too.

CHRIS

And Wham bars. You could go down to the sweet shop and get so many for your money.

STEPHEN

I know. Money seemed to last forever. My auntie Kit gave me 50p once and I went down to the shop and got a can of Coke, a bar of chocolate and some crisps. If ever I had a pound note I thought I was rich.

CHRIS

I used to spend all my money on Kinder Eggs. When they first came out they had this promotion where you could collect loads of different Donald Duck figures. Maria, Sharon and I were obsessed with them.

My dad paid me for doing some jobs for him and I spent all my money on Kinder Eggs. I didn't want the chocolate so I used to lob it at cars, but I desperately wanted to get the full collection of figures.

STEPHEN

Sticker albums were massive. Even though I wasn't into football I used to collect all the football stickers.

CHRIS

If you were a boy in the 1980s there was always one ear you had to have pierced, and that was the left one. I got the wrong ear pierced by mistake. But it's fitting because it's widely thought having your right ear pierced means you're gay. So the other kids told me.

STEPHEN

Who decided which was which? I got my ear pierced just before I started secondary school. My auntie Sheila gave me the money and I went down the market and got it done.

I had loads of piercings in my twenties. I had one in my chin, one in my nose, one in the little gristly inside bit of my ear and two in my eyebrow. I remember seeing my auntie Johna once and she said to me, 'I'm not talking to you until you take that stuff out of your face.' And she was true to her word.

One day when I was about 24 I looked in the mirror and thought, 'You look an absolute cock' and I took them all out. I never understand why girls put big bullrings in their nose. They look horrible. A little stud is fine but you don't want to look like you're about to be taken to market.

I can't bear the ear stretching. It makes me feel a bit sick. And everyone who has a tongue piercing seems to have this real need to let you know they've got it. They'll sit there talking to you playing around with it in their mouths. I deliberately don't mention it. People with tongue piercings are a bit like vegans. How do you know if someone is a vegan? Because they'll fucking tell you.

I tried to grow a rat's tail once because they were really in but I only managed one that was about an inch and a half.

CHRIS

We had a hairdresser on our estate called Jessie. Everyone used to go to her house and get their hair cut in her kitchen, or sometimes she'd come to our house. I always wanted to grow my hair, but as soon as it got to a decent length Jessie would come over and give me a crew cut.

I grew a really long rat's tail and I was so proud of. I refused to let Jessie near my hair when I had it because I was terrified she'd snip it off. My mum started cutting my hair instead and it was a disaster because she always cut my fringe way too short.

The first time I was allowed to get my hair cut in a proper salon I went to this place in town. We used to call it 'Tits and Bums' because that's all you needed to get a job there. It didn't matter if you could cut hair or not; as long as you had a good pair of boobs you were in.

All these really tarty women worked there and they were shit so I still ended up with really naff haircuts. I was really unlucky with my hair growing up. I think that's partly what inspired me to go into hairdressing.

Chapter Three

LiKE A ViRGiN

Chris: 'I still remember lying on my bed thinking, "I don't think I'll ever meet someone who wants me". I just wanted someone to love me. Even just *like* me. I felt so alone.'

STEPHEN

Is there anything worse in the world than puberty? I look at teenagers now and I envy their slimness and great skin but I would not want to have to go back to those awkward years for anything.

Puberty was hell for me. When we all had to have showers after PE at school I used to try and hide in the corner so no one could see me. All the other boys were hung like donkeys and really hairy and then there was me with a tiny, bald button mushroom between my legs. I felt like everyone was laughing at me, as if I wasn't self-conscious enough at that age already.

CHRIS

The first person to reach puberty in our year was a guy called Martin and he had a massive schlong. He was all manly and the rest of us were puny and he knew we were all jealous of him.

STEPHEN

But if I'd been him and I was the only one with hair and a dick I'd have felt like a freak.

CHRIS

Oh, he didn't care. He'd walk around showing his bits off really proudly.

STEPHEN

I was a late developer in every way and I felt like all the other boys in my year looked like Magnum compared to me. When I finally did start getting pubes I just got ten poker-straight hairs above my willy, which wasn't going to impress anyone.

CHRIS

And they were probably longer than your willy.

STEPHEN

They probably were. I didn't know about how your balls dropped or anything, so the whole thing was a mystery to me. Then at about 13 or 14 I got two little lumps in my nipples so it looked like I was growing boobs. I was shitting myself.

Because my dad wasn't around my mum got my cousin Tony to come round and give me a talking to about blokes' stuff. I showed him my nipples thinking he was going to laugh and say I had a future on Page 3 but instead he said, 'Nah, it's fine. They'll go soft and then they'll go hard again and it'll be alright.' What a bloody relief.

CHRIS

I didn't have that problem. Gutted. I would have loved it if I'd thought I was growing some tits back then. It would have been like all my prayers had been answered.

STEPHEN

I was such a late developer I would say I didn't have a full bush until I was 17.

CHRIS

I was a bit younger than that but I was never comfortable with myself and, like you, I hated having to get naked in front of everyone else. I loathed sports so much I used to forge my mum's signature on notes so I could get out of it.

I'd turn up for PE and the teacher would say, 'Oh, are you ill again? Well, that's a surprise.' He totally knew what I was playing at.

STEPHEN

I got so good at forging notes by copying my mum's signature I can still do it to this day. I'm an expert.

CHRIS

I hated school so much I used to say to my mum, 'I don't want to go today. I'll decorate a room if you let me stay off.' So I went through a phase of painting our house. I went back after having some time off once and matron said to me, 'Which room are you decorating at the moment?'

I started going to school less and less and by the time I was 14 the teachers was so desperate to make me go they paid for me to get a taxi there and back every day. But I hated it because I'd want to go out with my friends after school and instead I'd have to travel straight back home in a cab. Poor me, eh?

STEPHEN

Do you remember the nit nurse at school? What a weird concept. I used to love it when she came in to do the checks though. It was like getting a little head massage. And then there was the BCG. I didn't have that. I remember standing in the queue for it and everyone was coming out going,

'That bloody hurts,' so I thought, 'Fuck this' and I did a runner.

I hated lunchtime at school as well. Because we were poor we used to get dinner discs and I felt really embarrassed about it. The dinners were rancid but I loved the salty, soggy cabbage. Genuinely.

When I was about 15 I came up with a brilliant plan. Each dinner disc was worth 36p so I used to sell it for 20p and go down the chip shop. Chips cost 7p for a bag, and I remember being outraged when they went up to 7 and 1/2p.

If we weren't hungry my mates and I would club together and buy ten Number Ten fags for 54p and have them for lunch instead. Healthy.

CHRIS

I remember loving the blancmange at my school, but then for some reason they stopped school dinners altogether and I had to start taking a packed lunch and it was so miserable.

My mum used to make me Marmite sandwiches and there was always a thumbprint where she'd held the bread to cut it in half. Every day I'd take my sandwich out of the cling film and there would be this dent in the bread like she'd done it on purpose. I used to eat around the dent and throw the thumbed bit away.

My lunchbox always smelt funny when I opened it, too. Kind of musty. My drink would be warm and everything in there looked a bit limp. Everyone else's lunches always looked more appetizing than yours, didn't they? Someone always had a Wagon Wheel or something and I'd gaze longingly at it, dreaming of the day when I could buy as many as I wanted.

STEPHEN

I love kids' food now, and I love egg sandwiches most. We've got two shops near where I work where I can go and get a sandwich for lunch. Bob at the nice deli, Hampers, does a really posh egg and cress sandwich on granary bread. But sometimes I'll sneak past them and go to the bakery two doors down and buy a really filthy egg mayonnaise sandwich on white bread.

CHRIS

When I worked at Toni and Guy in central Brighton I used to get Steak Bakes from Greggs every morning for breakfast.

STEPHEN

You got me onto the sausage and bean pasties from there. They're so dirty. I always felt like I should go and hide down an alley to eat them.

CHRIS

A seagull nicked a pasty out of my hand when I was walking down the road a couple of years ago. I shouted, 'You bastard!'

really loudly in the middle of the street and I think people thought I was being mugged or something. I suppose I was, in a way.

This massive seagull shat on me the other day. I know it's supposed to be good luck but it didn't feel like it when it was dribbling down my clean top. They're like rats with wings those bloody things, but they do look quite cool and prehistoric too. We've got so many of them in Brighton.

STEPHEN

The worst thing about seagulls is when they start having babies. I used to live in a flat in Hove and my bedroom was in the eaves. The babies used to sit on my roof whining all bloody night and keep me awake. And when you're driving they sit in the middle of the road really arrogantly like they're daring you to run them over.

The problem is there's so much litter and food on the beaches these days that seagulls don't have to go out to sea to fish anymore so they're always pinching people's food. They drive me mad. You have to watch your dogs around them as well because they can pick small dogs up.

CHRIS

I don't know what I'd do if a seagull tried to steal Buddy or Rusty. I'd be so traumatized.

STEPHEN

I know. Can you imagine? Especially given how much we worship our pets. Dogs are so much better than people. My three toy poodles, Babs, Princess and Betsy, are my world.

I love taking them to the park because they make me laugh so much. Babs and Princess lap the park and fight with each other and Betsy stands there barking like the Cowardly Lion.

You can tell the time by Betsy because every night at 9pm she'll get on her back and stick her legs in the air and start barking her head off.

CHRIS

They do say that dogs are like their owners.

STEPHEN

People do look at me and think 'dog'. I've got one of those faces.

CHRIS

I was wondering the other day if I'm like Buddy and Rusty and I did think, 'Well I'm short and orange with a big nose'. But I don't wee and poo on the floor.

STEPHEN

My fiancé Daniel looks like our dog Babs with his curly gingery hair.

CHRIS

Pets do make a home, especially if you live on your own. They're always excited to see you.

STEPHEN

You can go off for a piss and when you come back into the room it's like they haven't seen you for ten years. They're like, 'Oh my gooooooood!'

CHRIS

Dogs don't have any sense of time though, do they? If you walk out of a room for five minutes they'll think you've been gone a day. I'll walk in after popping to the fridge and Buddy and Rusty will jump up and lick me like I've just been away on a two-week holiday.

STEPHEN

My first dog was called Kim and she was a Labrador. She died of old age and after that we got a whippet called Blue Boy. We got him from my Uncle Cyril because he used to race whippets, but Blue Boy was rubbish and he refused to chase the rabbit round the track so he had to retire very early.

Then Paul looked after a dog called Matty, who was a little Jack Russell. Then we had my Charlie, and then I got Alfie who was a Rottweiler cross Alsatian and he was massive. He went to live with some friends when I moved to London and I didn't have another dog until I got my three girls.

CHRIS

I feel like I've got a nice number now with Buddy and Rusty and my fiancé Tony's basset hound, Freddie. I would definitely have more if I could but where do you stop? I would keep on getting them until I was pushed out of my own home.

I've also got my cat I call Feral Beryl (real name Sherbert), but she's very shy. The only time she comes near me is when I go to bed and she'll come up and sit on my chest and purr and dribble on me. But the moment I go to stroke her she runs off like someone's put a rocket up her arse. She's a funny cat.

Buddy and Rusty have become local celebrities thanks to *Gogglebox* and they often get recognized before I do. When I'm out walking them people say to me, 'Oh my God, they look just like the dogs from *Gogglebox*!' Then they'll look up and see me and go, 'Oh.' It happens all the time. They're far more famous than Stephen and me. They're great little characters.

I got them because my friend has got a half dachshund, half Jack Russell called Ella and I love her. I said to Tony that if I ever got a dog of my own I'd get one like her, but a ginger version because I love red dogs.

I kept seeing faded red dachsies everywhere and one day Tony and I looked online and this advert popped up for red dachshunds. We drove all the way to Maidstone to see them that day. When we arrived the lady selling them handed one each to Tony and I and it was impossible to decide between them. And they're twins! They were actually born in the same bag. They looked identical back then and in the end I couldn't split them up. I hated the thought of them going through life not knowing their other half so Tony and I agreed we'd get them both.

From the moment I got the boys they changed my life. They were weeing and pooing on the floor constantly and we were getting woken up at 5am by howling, but I didn't mind because I adored them. They still do the odd excitement wee on the kitchen floor but they're absolute joys. I found out later that you're not supposed to get two dogs from the same litter because of this thing called 'littermate syndrome', where they can fight to be top dog. But they've been amazing. I love them so much, and they love each other.

Buddy is the leader of the pack and he's always the one in front when we go for walks, while Rusty lags behind. But Rusty can hold his own too. Freddie is the boss of both of them though. He may be an old chap at twelve years old, but he's in charge.

STEPHEN

My girls get on brilliantly. Princess and Babs do a lot together but Betsy likes to do her own thing. She'll hide a treat under a cushion, bark at it for hours, and then get it out again. She'll make her own entertainment. If we give them a treat Princess wolfs hers down straight away, Babs runs off with hers and then eats it and Betsy will carry hers around all day crying before she eats it.

CHRIS

If we give the boys treats Buddy's goes straight down in one gulp and Rusty takes his time to really enjoy his. Buddy looks so cross when Rusty is savouring his chew so he often tries to steal it. I'll look at him and say, 'That could have been you, Buddy!'

STEPHEN

Betsy will play with a piece of string and have the best time ever, and if we buy her anything fluffy she'll try and hump it. We bought her a big furry rabbit once and we had to take it away and hide it in a kitchen cupboard because she wouldn't stop hammering it. She used to sit there crying at the door like some poor war wife whose husband had gone off to fight.

CHRIS

I probably like dogs more but I do love cats too. I used to have an amazing one called Ginge who sadly died last year. I always do an open garden at home to raise money for charity and one day this scraggy ginger started roaming around the garden. He was skin and bone and covered in ticks and everyone kept saying, 'Why is that manky cat hanging around your house?' But I instantly fell in love with him. I could see past his matted fur and rotting teeth and thought he looked like Aslan from *The Lion, the Witch and the Wardrobe*.

I gave him some food and stroked him for ages, and after that I couldn't get rid of him. He came back every day and I fell more and more in love with him. My other cat, Pushka – who I named after a club night we'll talk about later – was getting really old so I was really nervous about introducing Ginge into the house. I did it very slowly and they became friends and Ginge soon became a proper part of the family. Then eight months later he went missing.

I went round asking all my neighbours if they'd seen him and one lady said she'd seen someone pick him up and put him in the back of a van. Thankfully she remembered the name of the company on the side of the van so I phoned the number and tracked him down. It turned out he hadn't been a stray at all, he was a runaway, and the original owner's daughter had picked him up and taken him back to her mum. I was devastated and when they let me go and say goodbye to him I was so upset.

Then two days later he turned up at my house again and we all agreed that it was better if he came and lived with me full-time. I had him for another two years after that and we had a lovely time together. He was such a clever cat. He used to high five me, and if I pretended to ignore him when we were sitting on the sofa he'd put his paw on my face to get my attention.

STEPHEN

He chose you, didn't he? He had to travel across a main road to get back to you but he obviously thought you were worth the risk.

I hate cats but I loved Ginge. Everyone thought the world of him. Sometimes animals just come along that you can't help but love.

CHRIS

Ginge was like a dog. Cats aren't usually faithful. They'll eat your food and then go to someone else's house to try and get more. But he didn't do that. He followed me around everywhere.

STEPHEN

My sister Denise had two cats and because she still lives in Holland she called one England and one Holland. Eventually they just stopped coming home. Then one day she spotted England in the street and he saw her and turned his back on her. She reckoned someone else must have been feeding them and taken them in because he'd put on a load of weight. See, no loyalty.

CHRIS

I did think about doing something with animals when I was a kid but I could never have become a vet or anything because you have to study for years and years and my concentration wasn't great.

I was really into art at school and I was always very creative, but that was about the only thing I liked because I felt like I could express myself.

STEPHEN

I enjoyed art and RE. I think it was the storytelling in RE I liked most because it was like watching *Jackanory*.

CHRIS

Stephen, don't pretend you were good at RE. Until quite recently you didn't know who came first – God or Noah.

STEPHEN

No, I said who came first *Jesus*, God or Noah? Or was it Jesus or Noah?

CHRIS

You're digging yourself a hole.

STEPHEN

It must have been God, and then Noah and then Jesus? I don't understand the whole Noah thing. If he needed one of each animal how would he know whether they were boys and girls? And if two camels had a baby female camel how is that camel going to have a baby? By doing it with her dad? And what if mum and dad had six boys and then mum died? Or what if one of the animals was gay?

CHRIS

If we all came from Adam and Eve aren't we basically shagging our brothers and sisters?

STEPHEN

Ewww. Despite being rubbish at it I did enjoy RE. And I was good at drama. My drama teacher really encouraged me. In fact, she encouraged me so much she convinced me to play Mary in the Nativity play at my all-boys' school.

She said to me, 'Stephen, you're the only person in this school that can do it.' And I felt so proud. I didn't have any lines but I had to sit at a table staring at a candle and looking pensive while someone else narrated. Then my husband came along. Who was I married to? Was Mary married to God? No, Joseph?

I was a bloody good Mary. I sat there looking out into the audience with a blonde wig on and everyone was staring at me open mouthed. I enjoyed the attention though. That was my moment in the spotlight. I was about 13 at the time. I wasn't, like, six or something.

CHRIS

So basically your starring role in life was pretending to be a woman in a non-speaking role? In a blonde wig? When Mary was dark haired?

STEPHEN

Yeah. But I totally pulled it off.

CHRIS

I always knew I was gay, right from when I was really young. Even at the age of five I knew I was different to other boys and I thought I was more like my sisters. I knew I was a boy but I thought I'd be a girl when I grew up. That was my way of dealing with how I felt.

I remember being in the woods near my house when I was about eight and I found a couple of pages that had been torn out of a porn magazine. They had both men and women on them and even then I thought, 'Well I like what he's got, but I don't like what she's got'.

And my bedroom was *far* too fabulous for a straight boy when I was a teenager. I had the coolest bedroom on the estate. I had a cast-iron bed with a mosquito net hanging over it, stars stencilled on the walls, a candelabra hanging from the ceiling and loads of scatter cushions. It was always tidy and I was always adding bits to it. I got an old wardrobe and stencilled all over it and it looked *fabulous*. This was in the days before Laurence Llewelyn-Bowen as well.

When I was about 13 I had blonde hair and guys would come over to me and say, 'My mate really fancies you,' and I'd be like, 'But I'm a *boy*.' Even then I was really girlie, and probably too pretty for a guy. My sisters used to dress me up all the time and I loved it. I'd find any excuse, but I used to make sure my parents didn't see me. Even now my sisters get annoyed by the fact that I was the prettiest one out of the three of us.

One time when I was about 14, I was lying on the sofa pretending to be asleep and Marie said to my dad, 'You do know Chris is *gay*?' and my dad replied, 'No he's not, he just likes female company.'

Obviously I hadn't talked to anyone about it at that point and I think Marie was just messing about. But it made me realize that I couldn't be myself in front of people because I *would* be judged. My dad was a proper old-school man's man and I knew he would find it incredibly hard if his only son was gay.

STEPHEN

I got my sister Beverley to do my make-up so I looked like a girl. When I looked in the mirror I could have cried because I was so ugly. It didn't suit me at all. I wasn't a man who suited make-up like Chris did.

CHRIS

It all left me feeling so confused though. I still remember so clearly lying on the bed in my boudoir as a teenager and thinking, 'I don't think I'll ever meet someone who wants me'. I just wanted someone to love me. Even just *like* me. I felt really alone.

I was so far in the closet at school I ended up sleeping with a girl just to try and get the bullies off my back. Everyone else knew I was gay before I did and, needless to say, losing my virginity was hilarious.

It was at a friend's house party and I'd had a few drinks and I knew this girl there liked me. All my mates had already lost their virginity and I was 17 and still hadn't had any kind of experience. It was one of those 'now or never' moments.

Me and this girl, who we'll call Louise, went upstairs to a bedroom and she was so excited at the prospect of getting off with me she practically had her clothes off the minute we walked in. We got down to it and I was halfway through when my friend's dad came home early and walked in on us. Louise and I were running around trying to grab our clothes and get dressed, and the dad was so furious about what we were doing in his house he started chucking all of our stuff out of the window. The whole of my town found out I'd lost my virginity because of that.

STEPHEN

That must have kept the homophobes at bay for a while though?

CHRIS

It did, but it also made me want to come out more than ever. Back then, my life was like the TV series *Beautiful People*. I was repressed and living on a council estate, dreaming about the day when I could grow up and move to London and live amongst the beautiful people.

I remember us having a get-together in my mum's living room when I was about 17 and I drank half a bottle of neat vodka. I liked a drink. I was completely off my head and I was lying on the floor and I snogged this guy called Jeremy. He was so gorgeous. Everyone was so shocked and all our mates were shouting, 'Oh my God, what are they *doing*? Quick, separate them!'

I woke up the next morning and the first thing I thought was, 'I snogged Jeremy!' I was *so* happy.

The gossip went racing round my estate and I made out I was so drunk I hadn't been aware it had happened. But all I wanted was for it to happen again.

I was out of luck though. Jeremy didn't speak to me for years after our snog and it was only a little while ago he got back in contact with me via Facebook. He's married with a kid now.

STEPHEN

Were you a big partier back then?

CHRIS

I wasn't crazy but we always had house parties round at mine because my sisters organized them Also, I think when my dad passed away my mum felt lonely and wanted us around more, so she used to arrange quite a lot of get-togethers.

I thought people were boring because they'd all sit on the sofa looking miserable while I was up dancing around. There was always trouble between my sisters' mates and often the police would get called at some point during the night.

The first time I got *properly* drunk I was 16 and my friend Lisa and I bunked off college. We got some really cheap cider and she gave me some hay fever tablets to give it that extra kick. We planned to go to London but we ended up passed out in Chesham train station waiting room, so someone called an ambulance and we were taken to High Wycombe hospital to have our stomachs pumped. Then we had to endure the hell of a long bus journey back to Chesham. That was definitely our punishment.

STEPHEN

Everyone always starts with cider in their teens, don't they? No one really liked cider or lager but you drink it because it's cheap.

CHRIS

I did all the usual teenage rebellion things back then. I really wanted to smoke and look cool so I went and bought myself ten fags because I wanted to fit in. But I was rubbish at it and had to give up before I'd even started.

STEPHEN

The thing about starting smoking is that you had to be sick at least two or three times before you properly got the hang of it. But once you master it the likelihood is you'll always be a smoker. I could give up tomorrow, but I know that several weeks down the line I'd be back on them. The longest I can go is about six weeks and then I'll start again. Once you've got yourself trained, that's it.

No one likes the tastes of fags when they first smoke. It's vile and it's so weird how we force ourselves to do it. You're lucky you never got the hang of it. I wish I'd never started.

I think 16 is a big year for a lot of people. You're starting to become an adult and you can legally do more things. It was the year I started fully understanding that I was gay and I hated it. I used to pray on my knees to God every night up until the age of 20 saying, 'Please make me straight. Please make me straight.' I hated those years.

I knew there was something up from the age of 12. At that age I was still climbing trees and making camps. I wasn't taking drugs and putting naked photos on Snapchat like kids these days. It was all so innocent and I didn't really know a lot about being gay. I just knew I had funny feelings towards guys.

I guess one giveaway was the fact that whenever my mum's new Kays catalogue arrived, I'd go straight to the men's underwear section and look at all the bulges. But I didn't really understand why.

I remember when the *Sun* started putting a topless man on Page 7. There was a man lying in these tiny swimming trunks, and I turned the page hoping I was going to see his bum. I still kept trying to convince myself I could be straight though.

I thought being gay was the worst thing in the world, especially as it was around the time the first AIDS adverts started appearing. There was one really hard-hitting ad of a gravestone with AIDS written across it in massive letters. That was absolutely terrifying. John Hurt did the voiceover and it was almost demonic. I was convinced that being gay meant I would get ill and die.

CHRIS

The AIDS campaign affected me so much. I remember guys asking me out when I was in my late teens but I was too scared.

STEPHEN

There were no other gay guys at my school so, like Chris, to try and be accepted, I went out with some girls. I had my hair cut into long curtains back then and for some reason the girls used to think I looked like Mark Owen so I was really popular.

Of course, I didn't want to have sex with the girls I was with so I used to pick the really nice, sweet girls that didn't want to get their knickers off. But even then, after three or four months they'd start thinking, 'Oh, come *on*!' So I'd dump them and go out with someone else. All the boys thought I was going through girls like nobody's business, but all these lovely, sweet girls were my early beards.

CHRIS

But you weren't getting any action at all back then? You didn't get down to it with any of them?

STEPHEN

I did actually sleep with a couple of them but I didn't lose my virginity until I was 17. I was at a house party and there were loads of boys but only three girls. I pulled one, my brother Paul pulled one and my friend Lee pulled the other one.

All the other boys were told to go home so the girls could get laid and we all went upstairs to the bedrooms. Me and this girl were in bed kissing and cuddling and we ended up having sex. It lasted about twenty seconds, tops. I was so shaky afterwards I went to the toilet and shit through the eye of a needle. It was the most horrifying experience of my life. Then when I went back upstairs my brother was in bed with her.

I got together with a girl when I was 21 and she asked me what my fantasy was. When I said, 'You, me and another girl,' she was well excited. And looking back, I'm pretty sure she was a lesbian. I don't think that relationship was going anywhere.

It got to a point where I couldn't fake it anymore. And I also didn't want to. But I had no idea how I was going to tell people this massive secret I'd been carrying around with me for years and years.

CHRIS

But it's not just a case of coming out, is it?

STEPHEN

Not where we were from.

CHRIS

The first person I came out to was my sister Sharon. She was fine about it, and probably not that shocked to be fair.

I was far more scared about telling Marie and my mum I was gay because it made it more final somehow. If they knew there was no going back.

I remember a guy called Mark, who was a friend of Marie, cornered me one day and said, 'I know about your dirty little secret and you had better run home and tell your mum and sister because I'm coming round later and if you don't tell them, I will.'

I was put in this really awkward situation where I had to go back and sit my mum and Marie down and say, 'There's something I need to tell you about me.' The first thing Marie said was, 'You've got a girl pregnant?' and then, 'You've robbed a bank?' After a few minutes of throwing out more random ideas she said, 'Oh, you fancy *boys* as well as *girls*?' Mum shook her head and said, 'Oh no, he's not one of *them*.' I knew it was a case of 'now or never' so I said, 'Actually, mum, I am. Except I don't like girls.' Mum paused for a moment and then went, 'Oh, is that it? Does anyone want a cup of tea?'

All of the pressure and fear I'd felt – as well as the frustration at being manipulated into telling my family – had all led up to that very un-dramatic moment. We didn't have a long discussion about it or anything. Everyone accepted it really quickly and I felt a huge sense of relief. And it wasn't long before word got around.

I only knew of two other guys in my school who were gay. But the thing was, they were liked and I wasn't, so even they used to take the piss out of me. It annoyed me that they were accepted and yet no one gave me an easy time of it. One of them was screaming from the heavens so it's not like he was closeted or anything. I don't know what it was about me?

I was always a bit of a loner growing up and then when I came out the friends I did have abandoned me. I felt like

I'd finally got a good group of people around me but when I told them all in no uncertain terms I was gay they all turned against me.

Julian and I stayed friends for a while but when I came out the closet I was too scared to tell him in case he didn't want to be mates anymore. He'd beaten a few people up for calling me gay, so when he eventually found out that I *was* gay he felt like he had to distance himself from me, and our friendship ended.

We didn't talk for about ten years but we got back in touch a while ago and met up and it was really nice. He turned around and said to me, 'I'm really proud of you because you've gone on to do so many things I've never done.'

After I came out and my mates turned their backs on me I felt like I didn't have much else to lose and that's when I started wearing girls' clothes more openly and really expressing myself. I started wearing make-up when I went out too, and my mum found it really hard. I guess she didn't know how to handle the fact that her only son could potentially become another daughter.

I was going through a lot and I really needed her support but we kept arguing about what I should and shouldn't do. One day we ended up having such a massive row we both slapped each other round the face and burst into tears. Then we both hugged and it was all forgotten. It must have been so difficult for her at times. It was a big thing for her to get her head around.

STEPHEN

Your mum is the same as my mum. She didn't get it then and I don't think she really one hundred per cent gets it now. It wasn't 'normal' for their generation to be open about their sexuality. I'm sure they've come to terms with it as much as they can but it will always be a little bit tricky. Mum fully accepts that I'm gay but it took a little while to realize it wasn't a phase.

I was 22 and living in London when I came out. I'd been seeing a South African boy called Daniel who was moving back home. I was feeling a bit down about it so I'd gone back to see Mum. I was sitting in front of the TV, writing Daniel a letter and Mum asked me who I was writing to. I said it was a mate of mine and she said, 'That's a fucking long letter isn't it?' and with that she went upstairs.

I followed her up and sat on her bed and said to her, 'Mum, that letter I'm writing isn't to a friend. It's to someone I've been seeing who's moving away and I'm really upset. But it's not a girl, it's a boy.'

She looked a bit confused and then said, 'Oh. Oh. Well, I don't know where you get that from because your father and me aren't like that. Well, I suppose it's up to you isn't it?'

I said I wanted to tell the rest of the family and she said, 'No, not just yet. Not until you know for sure.' Once I explained I *did* know for sure I called my sisters and arranged to meet them in the local pub so I could break the news. I just came out with it and they were genuinely surprised because they said they'd never suspected. I must have done a bloody good job of covering it up.

Now when I look back to my younger years I think if I hadn't been gay I'd still be stuck in my old life. But because I knew I wouldn't be accepted where I came from and I would never feel – excuse the cliché – free, I was forced to get out and get myself a life of my own. I had to go and find somewhere I'd feel like I fitted in.

If there is a God I think he made me gay because I had better things to do with my time than take drugs and go to prison, which quite a lot of people did. I think in some ways being gay saved me. If I'd been straight I'd definitely still be back in Sittingbourne with loads of kids, probably on the dole.

CHRIS

I never felt like I belonged anywhere as a kid so that was my motivation to get out and find somewhere I could be myself. Some of the kids I grew up with on the estate are still living there and bringing their kids up. Some of them have got grandkids living in the same house, which is crazy. At least we both got out and found our place.

When I was growing up I didn't think it was that obvious I was gay but looking back my mannerisms were, not to put too fine a point on it, quite feminine.

My sister's boyfriend had a video camera and he recorded us all messing about one day. He played it back on our TV a few weeks later and there was this girl sat on the sofa wearing a towel like a turban. I said to everyone, 'Who's that girl?' and they replied, 'That's you.'

My friend Maria came round one day and I'd just got out of the bath, so again I had a towel on my head. I opened the door to her and we sat chatting on the sofa for about ten minutes. When I took the towel off and she screamed and said, 'Oh my God, I thought you were Sharon!' She genuinely thought I was my younger sister.

I do think it's easier for gay people coming out these days. It's talked about so much more and there's so much more support.

I think once I'd taken that step to come out I felt like I may as well go all the way and talk to my doctor about the possibility of transitioning. I went and asked about starting hormone treatment to become a girl but he made me feel like a massive freak and I walked away feeling so dejected.

STEPHEN

A lot of people identify as bisexual now, don't they? It's not a big 'thing' anymore. And people are much more open about sexuality generally. Back in the day, if someone was gay everyone else would find out via word of mouth because it was a bit of a scandal and everyone would be gossiping. But now it's not a big deal. Not for most people, anyway.

CHRIS

In a way, I feel like we were cheated a little bit. We should have felt really privileged because it was still so much easier for people of our generation compared to our parents' one. But actually, now I think about it, it was still swept under the carpet a lot.

STEPHEN

Yeah, but at least we didn't go to bloody prison for it. It was illegal until the late 1960s. When you see gay people who are in their sixties or seventies now they must look at young people like us and think, 'You lucky bastards'.

I do wonder if I was protected by not coming out until later. If I'd come out at 16 and moved up to London I would have been a target for older men and I would have been very naïve. When I did come out, I had enough savvy in my head not to get led astray.

CHRIS

I can remember being 19 or 20 and having older guys coming on to me in clubs. I didn't lose my gay virginity until I was 21 and going out my first long-term boyfriend, Paul. I guess that's the time I should have been out there having fun and experimenting but it didn't feel right to me.

I love that I can say that I don't think young guys feel like they're on their own when they come out anymore. At least, I hope they don't. Whereas there were times in my teens when I felt like I was the only gay guy in the world. These days there are gay characters on TV programmes every day, but it was a really big deal when *EastEnders* got its first openly gay character, Colin, in the late 1980s, and I think things also started to change when Anna Friel had her lesbian kiss on *Brookside* in the early 1990s. It was just a kiss on a soap opera but it got people talking. Now we've progressed so much that loads of TV shows have got trans characters, which is great.

STEPHEN

We had a trans guy who lived on our estate. He was called Richard and he used to dress in women's clothes and call himself Tracy. Because we were horrible kids we used to call her Dick Tracy and torment her a bit.

She used to come down the road all dressed up and we'd say, 'Ooh, hello, Tracy!' and then piss ourselves. We didn't know any better and we thought it was funny. I do get why kids take the piss out of things they don't understand sometimes. But things are changing all the time.

I remember when Chris and I were in Ireland not that long ago and we walked past this group of boys. We were wearing tight skinny jeans and they openly laughed at us, I think because we looked gay to them.

CHRIS

I remember my ex-boyfriend's nephew telling me he was gay and that he was going to come out to all his friends at school. He was only 13 at the time but he felt so confident about it. When I was his age I felt absolutely petrified and it just shows how far things have moved on.

STEPHEN

There's so much out there on the internet for kids coming out now. There's loads of advice and help.

CHRIS

I think anyone who's coming out just has to do what's right for them, and I think the first step is always talking to a close friend or their parents if they can. It took me a while but I'm more comfortable with myself now than I've ever been.

STEPHEN

To me you've always been super-confident. You can walk into a room and talk to anyone. Not everyone's got that quality.

CHRIS

I've always been a bit worried about what people think, though. When I walked into my first job at Toni and Guy no one liked me because I came across as arrogant and overly confident, but I was the opposite so I was overcompensating.

STEPHEN

I was talking to my sister Sharon the other day and she said that over the years she's seen me become more and more confident with myself. She said it was at my sister Beverley's wedding that I first looked really settled with being who I am. And they think that's all down to you. I remember being quite jealous of you when we first got together because you were so comfortable with who you are.

There were some really macho people at Beverley's wedding and you were up dancing and completely being yourself and not giving a shit what anyone thought. Seeing you having such a good time made me think, 'Do you know what? I'm going to enjoy myself too. My family have got to see me for who I am.'

CHRIS

I don't think you had much choice when I was up on the dancefloor spinning my waistcoat round my head. I was almost doing a striptease.

STEPHEN

It feels like now you've got the confidence you want and you're mature and happy and you've got a nice house and a job. Even if it has taken a while to arrive.

CHRIS

I know. We should be like Benjamin Button and start off old and get younger. Loads of older people know what they want and they're really happy in themselves, but they don't have the energy to do all the things they want to do. But at least we can keep on having Botox.

Chapter Four

CRYSTAL BALLS

Stephen: 'What is déjà vu? It's weird, isn't it?'
Chris: 'It's like that film *Groundhog Day*.'
Stephen: 'Bollocks.'

CHRIS

It's funny how we don't realize how weird our teenage years are until we're out of them. Mine were such a roller-coaster and they were some of the best and worst times of my life.

One thing I really regret doing when I was a teenager is shoplifting. I used to nick things for people to try and make them like me. When I was 17 I got arrested for nicking blank cassettes. I was in a police cell for six hours and it scared me so much I never did it again. I'd much rather have no friends than be locked up.

STEPHEN

I was the same thing. I think all kids shoplift at some point, don't they? It was *always* either socks or blank cassettes that people stole. I always nicked socks. I have no idea why. I didn't even need them. I think I just did it for the thrill to see if I could get away with it, and because all my friends were doing the same. It was almost like a rite of passage. Not that I'm condoning it, obviously.

Back then you didn't have cameras everywhere and there was only one shop assistant working there, who was usually bored shitless and reading a book or something. Now there's CCTV bloody everywhere.

CHRIS

My saddest memory from my teens is of my dad dying when I was 15.

When I was 13 my dad's mum died. My dad had two sisters and a brother, but he was always her favourite because he cared for and looked after her so much. So when my nan passed away it had a huge impact on him. Nothing can prepare you for losing your mum. He wanted to give her a proper send off and she had no savings so he got a loan to pay for it. As a result, he had to work loads of overtime.

My dad was really stressed all the time and he didn't have a very healthy lifestyle because he was a big smoker. I think a combination of things caused him to have a stroke, which thankfully he recovered from.

But he still had his debts to pay off so he had to go straight back to work and really soon afterwards he had another massive stroke, which left him paralysed on his right side. He had to take early retirement and he lost the ability to speak properly and it was so hard to see him like that.

He was always such a protector and provider and I hated seeing him in that state. My mum is a very strong woman and she's always been a grafter so she always ran the house and kept the family together. But there was even more pressure on her when he became ill.

The evening before my dad passed away he seemed really well and happy. He'd been to visit his best friend Pete to have a few drinks. They'd been friends since they were teenagers and he wanted spend the night talking about old times.

He's planned to go fishing the following morning and when mum went to wake him he was already dressed and downstairs, which was unheard of. He was jokingly shouting up to my mum, 'Come on, woman. Get up and make me a cup of tea!' Mum went downstairs and as she was clearing up some mess in the kitchen she heard this massive bang behind her. When she turned around my dad was on the floor.

Sharon, Marie and I were woken up around 7am to the sound of mum screaming dad's name and begging him to wake up. We rushed downstairs and saw my dad lying on the floor. We called an ambulance but it was too late to save him.

I was so angry because he didn't have much support from his family and I honestly believe that if my dad hadn't been under such a massive amount of pressure money-wise he would never have had that first stroke, which led to the second, and finally the third one.

The funeral costs ended up causing disagreements within our extended family and I felt very angry towards them. As a result, I changed my surname from my dad's family name, Bradbury, to Steed, which is my mum's maiden name.

I had to toughen up and be there for my sisters. I only remember crying once when my sisters cried because I felt like I had to be strong. My mum didn't cry until a few days after the funeral. We were sat watching TV together and all of a sudden she broke down and that was it. Once she started she couldn't stop.

We pulled together as a family and I guess in some ways it made us stronger as a unit because we had to support each other, but it was such a terrible time. It feels weird to think that my dad's been dead longer than I knew him for. He hasn't been here for the last 25 years of my life now, which feels very odd.

To this day I wonder if he was proud of me because I knew he always wanted a proper 'boy' for a son, and that just wasn't me. I tried to do things like fishing and ferreting and hunting with him but I knew I could never be what he wanted me to be. When my nephew, Nico, who's now 21, came along, we always said that my dad would have adored him because he was such a lad.

I always remember my dad coming home with fish or rabbits after he'd been hunting. Mum would make rabbit stew and me and my sisters refused to eat it. Dad and I were miles apart in some ways, but I still feel like we had a good bond. He was always out working or at home watching westerns, so I suppose we didn't have a lot in common. I only really like westerns that have got Doris Day in them.

I do hope my dad's looking down on me and thinking that I've done alright for myself. I really do.

When my dad died I inherited all his jewellery and mum kept it for me until I was older and then I went on holiday to Thailand and my house got robbed while I was away. Some bastards stole the lot. So I don't have anything of my dad's anymore.

STEPHEN

That must have been a really awful time. And it must have been when you were doing all your exams at school, which is a lot of pressure anyway.

I eventually had it out with my dad for fucking off when we were kids, but not until I was in my thirties. I sent him a letter explaining exactly what had happened to us after he left. He got in touch and asked me to go over to Holland so he could explain everything.

When I arrived at his house we sat in the garden and I was sitting on a chair that was higher than his so I felt like I was looming over him. It was a really strange dynamic.

It was a long and difficult conversation. It was clear that his decision to leave had haunted him for years and he still doesn't sleep well. That made me feel bad, but I couldn't feel sorry for him. I wouldn't swap places with him for all the tea in China.

In a weird way I admire him for going off and chasing his dream. He got a smallholding, which is what he'd always wanted to do. But on the other hand, he left four kids in a shithole. How can you live with that? I did forgive him after that meeting, though.

We also talked about my brother Paul's death five years previously. He died twelve years ago from a heroin overdose and it's something my family will never get over.

When we were kids Paul was always getting into trouble. We smoked our first joint together in our local park when I was nine and he was ten. I didn't feel any different and I said to him, 'It's done nothing for me and if you do it again I'm telling mum,' and then minced off home. He came back an hour later and I was sitting in my bedroom with my headphones on rocking back and forth.

That was the first time I'd heard of or experienced drugs, but Paul was a law unto himself and as he got older he started to experiment more. He lived how he wanted to live and he didn't want to conform. We used to go to school for morning registration and then run off to the nearby orchard and hang out there until lunchtime. We'd go back to school to have some lunch, and we'd stay for afternoon registration and then go again. We were little buggers.

As we got older, Paul started to get into trouble with the police, and he also started doing harder drugs. We found out he was smoking heroin when he was in his mid twenties. He met a girl and had three kids and he packed the drugs in. But when they split up he went back to it and he began using needles.

Paul and I got on really well when we were kids but in our teens we really clashed so I didn't see him a massive amount in our twenties. I was living in London and he was still back at home. I think by the time he got to about 30 things were going steadily downhill and he'd almost given up on himself.

I'd moved down to Brighton by this time and my flatmate Lorna came into my bedroom and told me there was a message from my sister Sharon on our answerphone and she sounded really upset. I called her and she said to me, 'Paul's dead.' I was so shocked I fell to the floor. He was only 32.

We had to ID him but my mum was living in Blackpool then so Beverley's boyfriend drove down there to pick her up. Lorna drove me to the hospital and Sharon and Beverley met me there, but Denise was still travelling over from

Holland at that point. We were asked to identify him from behind a glass screen. I remember saying to the coroner, 'Why is he so brown? He's only just come out of prison?' It's weird what goes through your head at stressful times.

The coroner said that there was such a huge amount of heroin in his system that she didn't think he'd done it by mistake. He'd been taking heroin for many years and he would have known that amount would be fatal. He also had a litre of whiskey in him. She explained that he would have gone to sleep and his heart would have got slower and slower until it eventually stopped, so he didn't feel any pain. That was a little bit of a comfort.

Once we'd IDed him we all walked up the hospital corridor together. Paul was always clearing his throat and Beverley suddenly said, 'I'd give anything to hear him snort again.' We all started laughing and then burst into tears. The coroner must have thought we were mad.

We made sure he had an amazing send off and I must admit that my dad did step up and offer to pay for the funeral. In the end we divided it between all of us.

I got up and did a really long speech about how I didn't think Paul and I were that close, but actually we shared so many memories. All the things we did when we were kids came flooding back. We used to carry a bit of old lino and a boogie box around with us and do breakdancing, and we'd build camps and wind each other up all the time. So in reality, we were really close and we did love each other a lot.

My mum, my sisters and I still talk about Paul a lot. His birthday is always really hard for my mum but we will speak about him. I do hope at some point there will be more help for people with drug problems because quite often there is some kind of mental health issue involved as well. I wish we could find a better way to support addicts that didn't just involve them being given methadone.

CHRIS

I can't imagine how hard that must have been for you all. I do think it's a really positive thing that you were able to talk to your dad and get everything out in the open though. That was a really brave thing to do.

STEPHEN

It wasn't the easiest thing I've ever done but I'm glad I did it.

I left school at 16 without any qualifications at all and the first full-time job I had was at a pie factory where I made pastry. I hated it. I had to do shift work, so I worked from either 6am until 2pm, or 2pm until 10pm. Funnily enough, my mum worked in the same factory years before. But when she worked there it was a shirt factory and she did collars and cuffs.

I thought it was a crap place to work and I was only on £56 a week, but I stayed there for two years until I was 18 and could save a little bit of money. One good thing about the job is that the Inland Revenue got in touch with me recently to tell me that I'd opened a pension when I was 16 and it's now worth nearly ten grand. I can't draw on it until I'm 55 but at least it's there ready for a bloody nice holiday.

CHRIS
Was working at the pie factory the start of your eating downfall?

STEPHEN
It probably was to be fair. After I left there I worked in a few pubs and kitchens and then I worked in a petrol station, which I fucking loved. I used to sit on a chair with my feet on the counter taking the money and eating whatever I wanted. My mum always said to me, 'Just do whatever pays you a wage. You need money.' So I went from job to job.

I worked at the petrol station for about a year and a half and then I hit a low and signed on. I found that hard because I'd always worked for what I wanted. Even when I was about 13 I went hop picking and plucked turkeys.

My uncle Cyril was a real character and he used to take me and Paul down to this battery farm where he worked every Sunday to collect eggs. He'd drop us off, fuck off down the bookies, and then come back once we'd finished. He'd only have the chickens for a certain amount of time. Then they'd get taken off to be made into nuggets or something and he'd get a new lot in.

CRYSTAL BALLS

One day this new lot came in and he noticed this really fat chicken in one of the cages. He got this big one out and he called it Sargeant and he used to feed it special food. Sargeant used to walk up and down the rows of chickens keeping an eye on them and whenever she turned into a new lane they would all go completely silent. Then as soon as she went to the next lane they'd start clucking again. It was so weird.

A few months later another new load of chickens came in and when someone came to pick up the old ones they took Sargeant with them. Cyril was gutted.

After he got bored with eggs he set up a bread stall on the side of a dual carriageway. Again, he used to drop Paul and me off there and come back a few hours later. He'd take all the money and drop us off home with an iced bun and a quid as payment.

CHRIS

That's like child labour. You wouldn't get away with that now.

STEPHEN

I know, but we quite liked it. We felt like we had our own shop, which every kid wants, don't they? Cyril used to have a full English breakfast every day of his life, without fail, and he was skinny as a rake and lived until he was 79. It just goes to show, doesn't it? You've got to live your life and hope for the best.

Uncle Cyril was married to my mum's sister Johna and he was always round our house. Even though he was a strange bloke at times he was also like a father figure to us in some ways. He used to tell us that all the girls would be actresses and Paul and I were going to be famous directors. I used to think, 'I don't want to be a director, I want to be an actress'.

Mum was ill once when we were kids so we phoned Cyril and Johna and they arrived 20 minutes later. Cyril took one look at mum and said, 'Get me some margarine.' I went and got the tub from the fridge and Cyril sat there at the bottom of mum's bed rubbing margarine on her feet. He kept saying, 'Are you feeling better yet, Pat?' Fuck knows what he thought it was going to do. Baste her back to health?

Half an hour later Cyril got bored so he and my auntie buggered off home and left my mum lying there feeling just as shit, with really greasy feet.

CHRIS

There are some people you know as a kid that leave such an impression on you. My mum's friend Betty was a real character and she's someone I'll never forget.

She had really frizzy hair and looked like a female version of Ken Dodd. She was psychic and predicted that I was going to work for Toni and Guy. We always invited her to house parties and she'd start doing predictions for us, but she'd drag it out for ages. She spent so long saying,

'Something's coming through,' she never actually got to the point so we were all on tenterhooks.

STEPHEN

I've been to see psychics before but I've never seen one who's convinced me to totally believe in 'something else'. I went to this one who lives near me for a reading a couple of years ago and I still see her in the street sometimes. She always says to me, 'Are you going away travelling?' like she's making a live prediction and I'm like, 'No, I'm going to work, love.' And sometimes she'll say, 'Are you doing more TV work?' when I'm in the middle of filming a series of *Gogglebox*.

CHRIS

A friend of mine told me about this Tarot reader and when I went along she was shit. She said there was a really strong woman coming through from the other side saying she'd forgiven me. For what? I had no idea what she was talking about. Now I'm worried I said something terrible to someone when I was drunk and don't remember.

STEPHEN

I went to a medium once who told me she had an older lady with grey hair who smelt of lavender coming through to give me a message. I mean, come on, that could be anyone. Old women always have grey hair and smell of lavender. And wee.

CHRIS

I have to say, I did go and see one psychic a couple of years ago who was really good. He said to me, 'You're going to meet someone at the end of year. I can see two guys around you. One of them is younger and good looking and you're going to be mesmerized by him. But be careful because he can be hard work and he'll be trouble if you get involved with him. There's also a very handsome older guy. You already know him and he's ideal for you.'

Sure enough, that November I met this young guy who was a friend of a friend and an Olympic swimmer. He was very handsome with an amazing body but a bit of a Jack the lad. Then I met my wonderful Tony and sure enough I *did* already know him because our paths had crossed several years before. So sometimes I think people do have a bit of a gift. But equally, if someone tells you you're going to get a new job you may start looking for one just because they've said you will. So predictions can also shape your life, which I don't think is a good thing. At the end of the day, we've all got free will.

STEPHEN

The thing is, when you're in a good relationship and you've got a good job and you're happy you wouldn't even think about going to see a psychic, so I think it can be easy to pick up on things people are worried about. Don't we all get anxious about the same things? But, having said that, it can be very therapeutic and it's quite nice to spend an hour just talking about *you*. Who doesn't enjoy that?

CHRIS

I get déjà vu a lot. I always think when that happens it's because whatever's going on at that time has happened to me before. I feel like I know the outcome to something before it's happened.

What annoys me about déjà vu is that you don't realize it's déjà vu until after it's happened. Why don't you realize a couple of minutes beforehand so you can tell people what's going to happen? It always happens when it's happened. And you think, 'Oh, it's happened'.

STEPHEN

This is all doing my head in a bit. What is déjà vu? It's weird, isn't it?

CHRIS

It's like that film *Groundhog Day*.

STEPHEN

Bollocks.

CHRIS

I believe that we're all existing for a reason. I don't know what that is yet.

STEPHEN

I don't think anyone really knows what the meaning of life is, do they? For me it's just about having a good time. You've got to make the most of it and have as much fun as you can.

CHRIS

Try and be the best person you can be. Be good to those around you, treat people how you would like to be treated, and be kind.

STEPHEN

And have a fucking party. I don't think there's any really deep meaning behind any of it. I think when you kick the bucket that's it, you're worm food.

CHRIS

I think we do live on.

STEPHEN

Nah, totally not. I don't think there's any point to all of this. You're given a life, you live that life, and then you're off.

CHRIS

Why don't I kill you and then you can come back and haunt me and tell me what's happening?

CRYSTAL BALLS

STEPHEN

The whole point of life is to enjoy it. It's a precious thing. It's a gift. I don't believe the whole thing about people seeing lights when they have near-death experiences either. It's drugs. When you're in that state your brain produces that sensation. I'd like there to be something after this world but I don't reckon there is.

CHRIS

I like to think that I'll go on.

STEPHEN

And do what? Where are you gonna go?

CHRIS

I could live again.

STEPHEN

Think about it rationally. When you're dead and lying on the floor you're a corpse. Dead. You're just a bit of old rotting meat. So all that's left is your soul that inhabited that body.

CHRIS

And that can go on to live in another body. I'd like to come back as a girl. I'd be a right slag!

STEPHEN

No. No. Maybe we float around a bit but that's about it.

CHRIS

How do you explain past-life regression?

STEPHEN

It's a load of old shit! Nah. Why be so concerned about previous lives or the next life? Why not enjoy the one you've got?

CHRIS

I love history and if I could go back to any period in history it would be the Georgian era. Brighton and Hove became really fashionable in the Georgian period. There was a lot of glamour back in those days. It was quite gaudy and I love a guy in britches and boots. I wouldn't have lived in poverty though. I would have been part of the gentry or a really glamorous lady. I'd be dressed up like something out of *Hello Dolly*.

Tony and I love going to visit old houses and museums. I like seeing how far we've come. There's an amazing place in Brighton called the Regency Town House, which they've restored to how it would have looked originally. And I love Brighton Pavilion. I'm fascinated by how far we've come.

Do you know why women used to have bouquets on their wedding day in the olden days? It wasn't because they looked pretty, it was because everyone smelt so bad. Can you imagine how bad someone smelt in the height of summer? I live in a place called Hangleton and it's called that because they used to hang people up there. They used to put people in cages once they were dead and birds would come along and peck at them, and to this day there are still loads of birds in that area.

STEPHEN
Oh, tell me more.

CHRIS
I will! Do you know why a funeral wake is called a wake? It's because hundreds of years ago people used to drink out of cups that were made of metal. Alcohol reacted with the metal and they used to go into these coma-like states, but people assumed they were dead. Gravediggers discovered that they may have been burying people alive because they found scratch marks on the inside of some coffins.

To stop it happening again families wanted to make really sure their loved ones had passed away before they had a funeral. So they used to lay the body in the middle of a table and they'd all sit around it and eat and wait to see if that person woke up. Hence it's called a wake.

And do you know where the terms 'the night shift' and 'saved by the bell' come from? Just to make sure people were dead, funeral parlours would tie a bit of string to someone's big toe in the coffin and attach it to a bell. Someone would have to sit there all night and wait and see if any of the bells rang. If a bell rang they'd open up the coffin and get them out.

STEPHEN

Is that really true?

CHRIS

No, I just made it all up. Of course it is! What annoyed me about history at school was that it was always about war. Our teacher was quite sexy so I didn't mind the classes but I hated having to try and remember dates and stuff.

STEPHEN

I'm fascinated by war. It springs from my nan. When I used to go over to her house she'd play 1940s music and she talked about her husband, who she lost in the war. They had eight kids in total and he got leave to see their baby Miah when he was a couple of months old. He went back to fight and he was on the White Cliffs of Dover working as a gunner when he got killed.

My mum came along a few years later after my nan had a bit of a fling.

I've got so much respect for that generation. Seventeen-year-old boys were going off to fight for our freedom. If it wasn't for them we'd all be talking German now. I get to live my life and be openly gay and I think it's all thanks to that generation. I enjoy watching films like *The Bridge on the River Kwai* and *The Dam Busters* and reading books and learning about it all.

I'm one hundred percent behind the Help for Heroes charity because I'm just in awe of them all.

CHRIS

If there are other worlds and paradise exists somewhere I'd get a *whole* day off from working. I don't think that's too much to ask.

STEPHEN

And I'd be eating chips every day and not putting on any weight. Look, if there was life after death there are members of my family who have passed away that I'm convinced would have got in contact. I'm pretty positive my nan would have done. I'm sure someone would have come through.

CHRIS

But you don't know, do you? Some people are open to it. Are you open to it?

STEPHEN

Yeah, I would be.

CHRIS

I don't think you would. You've got to really believe to get messages. You don't think life after death even exists.

STEPHEN

When we went to Buckingham Palace and stood near the Queen, I must admit I did look up to the sky and think, 'I wonder if my old nan can see me?' and I did get a warm feeling over me. She would have been *so* proud because she would never have dreamed one of her grand-children would set foot over those gates. But still. . . nah.

CHRIS

But what about things like Stonehenge? That's weird. It's basically a big clock, isn't it? And they didn't even know about time back then, which is why some people think it was put there by aliens.

I don't know if I believe in aliens but there must be something else out there. I'm sorry, it can't just be us. You're not telling me we're the top of the food chain and that we're 'it'. And there must be something that's more intelligent than most humans.

Although, if there is a parallel universe I don't think there's a better-looking version of me living there because how could there be? I'm already hot enough.

CRYSTAL BALLS

STEPHEN

Apparently those rocks at Stonehenge were dragged from Wales. Do you think the aliens were Welsh?

I think if there was intelligent life on other planets they would have reached us by now. So if there are other life forms out there they may be a bit thick. It's worrying that they may not be as clever as humans, because, apart from Stephen Hawking, we're not the brightest, are we? When I think about the fact that we're just this little planet spinning around in space it scares me.

And the whole thing about Area 51 is a bit ridiculous. If there were such things as aliens they wouldn't just keep landing there, would they? Why wouldn't they land on the top of a multistorey car park and go to McDonalds?

CHRIS

I think ghosts are from a different time to us. I think we're all going along at the same speed but we're on different planes and sometimes there's a slight crossover.

STEPHEN

What the fuck?

CHRIS

It makes sense in my head. We could be sat somewhere and all of a sudden we could see someone walk through the room, because in their own time they are walking through the room. I don't think they're coming to haunt us; I think it's just when time overlaps.

STEPHEN

I think you've watched *Interstellar* too many times.

CHRIS

What do you reckon dreams are? I have really weird ones sometimes. Sometimes I wake up in the middle of the night and I think, 'That was such a good dream' and I tell myself I must remember it. Then I'll go back to sleep and when I wake up in the morning I can't remember it.

  I had a dream where I was Jennifer Aniston and a new world was being created around me. People were building everywhere and creating this internal world. Then I realized they were doing it in my garden.

STEPHEN

I get into bed most nights exhausted and it will take me about an hour and a half to go to sleep. Daniel is off as soon as his head hits the pillow, like Cinderella. He has nothing to worry about. He's never even had a parking ticket, whereas I lie there thinking about things for ages. If something's on my mind I can be awake all night.

CRYSTAL BALLS

CHRIS

Anyway, you may be cynical about spooky stuff but Betty said I'd be a hairdresser and she was right. Even if I did think it was a load of old shit when she first told me.

I went to art college straight out of school but the teachers kept going on strike so I didn't achieve what I wanted to because there was never anyone to bloody teach us. My plan was to become an architect or a designer of some kind and I went and did work experience in this design company every week to try and learn that way. In the end, the teaching situation was so crap I decided to drop out and try and get a job instead of wasting my time. Only two people on my course actually finished it and they probably learnt bugger all.

I went and signed on while I went job hunting, but I only did it once because when I stood in the queue at the job centre for the first time I thought, 'This isn't for me'. So I didn't do it again.

I had no idea what I wanted to do with my life. When I was at school I went through phases of wanting to do all kinds of different things. I wanted to be a policeman for a while when I was really young and I had this plastic helmet I used to wear all the time. But my dad told me I wouldn't be tall enough because back in those day you had to be about six foot to be a copper, so that was out of the question. I'm only five foot seven now.

It's weird that I wanted to go into the police force because

I was scared of policemen. Back then everyone was. I hated my dad smoking so I hid my dad's tobacco tin once and he pretended to call the police. I was only about seven and I ran up to my room and put loads of stuff in front of the door so the police couldn't get in to arrest me. My dad got my sister to go out the back door and run round and knock on the front door so I thought they'd arrived to take me away. I was shitting myself. My dad loved playing jokes on me.

Anyway, I was feeling really directionless work wise and then when I was 19 my mum said to me, 'I've always thought you'd make a really good hairdresser.' I replied, 'Mum, they're thick.'

STEPHEN
Pot, kettle.

CHRIS
It did get me thinking. I had no idea what else I could do so I thought 'Why not?' A few days later me and my friend Paula walked from Chesham to the next town, Amersham. It's a few miles and it took us bloody ages.

I walked into a hairdressers, Profile, and the manager said he'd happily take me on and train me up. How amazing is that? It was that easy for me to get a job.

I stayed at Profile for about six months and I got really friendly with a girl who worked there called Brenda. She was pissed off with a few things that were happening there and she wanted to leave, so one day she convinced me to walk out with her. I was young and impressionable and she was my best friend so I went with it. I thought I was being rebellious and I wasn't thinking about the consequences.

We both got jobs working for a company called MediClean, which involved cleaning Amersham Hospital. They put me on the psychiatric ward.

STEPHEN
Funny that.

CHRIS
It was properly scary. I coped with it for two days and then I asked to be moved. I got put on the old people's ward, which was just as bad. I was cleaning the floor and all of a sudden I heard the death rattle from some poor old bloke. I lasted a day.

Brenda was cleaning all the staff quarters and she said to me, 'It's a fucking doddle. I just lie on the bed and watch TV all day.' I managed to wangle my way in and I worked there for a day and I was bored senseless. Brenda and I had a big fallout, and the following week I went to Profile and grovelled for my job back.

I was totally broke but loved being back at the salon. I really put in the work and within a few years I was running the technical department of three salons. I felt amazing.

This was also around the time I started properly going out. I had a whole new group of friends and began going out clubbing locally.

One night I was in this club dancing like mad (whilst wearing tartan trousers) and some guy came up and started dancing behind me. Apart from Jeremy, that was the first time I'd ever been that close to a guy and I didn't quite know what to make of it. But I knew I liked it. Sadly it turned out he was drunk and straight and his mates came and dragged him away from me.

I started to realize that I was never going to meet the man of my dreams in Chesham, and I'd have to branch out a bit if I had a hope of ever getting a snog with another guy. I'd never been to a gay club before so I arranged to go up to Heaven, which was London's biggest and best gay club, with a load of my friends one Saturday. We all went to a bar called Halfway to Heaven, which was just around the corner from the club, and then all my mates decided they were tired and they wanted to go home.

I was, quite literally, steps from Heaven, so I was absolutely gutted. It was my dream to go to a gay club and it was being cruelly snatched away from me. Then there was a shining light at the end of that tragic tunnel. My mates started talking to these two gay guys called Jamie and Adam and they offered to take me to Heaven (literally). They could see how disappointed I was so they said I could hang out with them for the evening and stay at their flat. I didn't need to be asked twice.

The minute I walked into Heaven I felt as if all my dreams were coming true. I was like a kid in a sweet shop. It was such an eye-opener and I was mesmerized by all these guys who were gay JUST LIKE ME.

I walked around taking everything in and after a lot of drinks I snogged a few random guys. I rounded the night off by having a bit of a snog with Jamie; even though it turned out he was seeing Adam.

I believe Jamie and Adam didn't last very long and Jamie and I started casually dating each other. He even took me on a dirty weekend to Worthing.

STEPHEN

Worthing? What a treat. He didn't even take you to Brighton?

CHRIS

It was only because he had a relative who lives in Worthing so we went and stayed at her place. We did go out in Brighton though. It was the first time I'd ever been and I instantly knew I wanted to live there one day. It was one of the coolest places I'd ever been.

The more I went clubbing the more outrageous my hairstyles and clothes got. I had bright copper hair with a long fridge and a blonde streak. There's a photo of me somewhere wearing a shiny satin blouse, tiny glasses, full-blown make-up and I've got really long nails. That's how I walked around on a day-to-day basis. I looked like a female version of Harry Potter crossed with Dennis Pennis. With long nails.

I was always going to themed events at a club night called Pushka. They were once a month and in between that I'd go to Heaven and other clubs in central London. Heaven was fantastic back then. I was always up on podiums dancing away. My friend James and I used to plaster on fake tan before we left the house and then we'd both wear white vests. By the time we came out of a club we'd have orange marks all over our vests from where we'd sweated all our fake tan off.

One week they had a hats, wigs and tiaras theme and my friends said to me, 'Can you tone it down this week? You always wear things that are so over the top.' Of course I said yes. I didn't want them to feel embarrassed.

I based my outfit around my mum's beautiful wedding tiara. I had bleached blonde hair then and I put silver wax in it and moulded it into points. I put the tiara on, added a silver, glittery vest, white bell-bottomed trousers and some massive silver platforms. I painted my nails silver and did really natural-looking make-up with silver eye shadow so I looked like an ice queen. When my friends arrived to pick me up I threw on a white fur coat and walked out the house shouting, 'I'm heeeeeere!' They were horrified. I had the best night. I got so much attention. I could party all night back then.

CRYSTAL BALLS

My plan was to be as 'out there' as possible so people were too scared to talk to me. It was a real defence mechanism because I was still worried someone was going to give me a hard time for being gay.

I looked so strange that at times people would cross the road, walk past me, and then cross back over because they didn't want to walk on the same side of the street as me. That's how small-minded and backward my town was.

STEPHEN

To be fair, if I saw you with copper hair and a shiny blouse now I'd cross the fucking street. Did you look like Lynda La Hughes from *Gimme Gimme Gimme*?

CHRIS

Yes, but much sexier.

Chapter Five

LiVE AND LET DYE

Chris: 'My friend Gary said to me, "Ditch the hair and the make-up and be a boy. Or have your willy cut off and become a girl. You can't have it all."'

CHRIS

I eventually moved out of home when I was 21. My sister Marie kept moving out and coming back home, and one day I heard her say to my mum, 'Why don't you chuck Chris out? He needs a bit of independence.' We had a big row about it because I said I wanted to be financially independent first.

I wanted to stay in Chesham near my family and work, and once I made the leap I loved standing on my own two feet. My mum was gutted though, because the house always looked tidier when I was around.

I wasn't scared of being on my own because I've always been a grafter. I just got on with stuff. And I started going out in London more and more. I'd take a bag of clothes in with me on a Friday and my workmate Lisa and I would get ready in the salon, get the train to London, go clubbing all night and get the first train back. We'd go to McDonalds on the way to work and get a giant fizzy drink for the sugar rush to perk us up. Then I'd do a full day in the salon, go back to London and do it all again.

I used to wear some amazing outfits. I remember going to Ministry of Sound in these massive black platforms, black hot pants and a bright red crop top that said 'Enjoy Cock' on it, written like the Coca-Cola slogan. I had short blonde hair and I was on the dancefloor giving it some while all these guys grinded up against me thinking I was a girl. I was so skinny back then.

When I look back I can't believe what I wore. I was often going out dressed as a girl now, but to be honest it felt tame compared to some of my clubbing looks. My alter ego Christina evolved as time went on. I suppose I first properly discovered her when I was 13 and I started putting make-up on and growing my hair and experimenting. Then when I came out I got much bolder, and she kept reinventing herself as the years went on. By the time I was in my twenties I had perfected my look and I got so good at dressing up people didn't realize I was a bloke. Straight men used to flirt with me all the time.

I remember standing on the glass bridge in Ministry of Sound wearing a really fitted green dress and a long, blonde wig. I looked down and all these guys were trying to look up my skirt. I was all strapped down so no one was any the wiser, and they'd walk past me and flirt.

I did look great when I really dressed up though. I used to buy a lot of Christina's clothes from Morgan, Topshop and Miss Selfridge. It was ridiculous because I used to spend a fortune on Christina and then skimp on my own clothes. I'd buy her a £200 pair of boots but I'd think twice about buying a £30 pair of trainers for the gym. But in my eyes she was worth it because she was perfect. She was properly spoilt.

STEPHEN

I remember walking into Heaven and thinking, 'Fuck, I'm not the only one! There's a room full of men I'm in with a chance with!' That was when I started to think it may be okay being me after all. I'd kept things hush-hush until then. But that night changed everything.

Apart from Poofy Dave, the first time I met someone who was gay was when I was 20 on a night out in London. I'd never been to London before so I got the train from Kent to Victoria and headed for Embankment. I had no clue where I was going but somehow I managed to stumble across Heaven. It was like someone from above was guiding me.

After going clubbing in London a few times I knew that was where I had to be. I'd just come back from a stint in Holland growing tomato plants in a greenhouse and getting stoned. I used to drive around on this little electric trolley debugging plants and smoking weed. It was a lovely job and my sister Sharon worked up the road in cucumbers, while Denise worked in roses a bit further up from her. I had such a great time but I knew I couldn't do that forever.

So I was back living at home, signing on, I had no money and no place of my own. I was going nowhere in a hurry. All my friends were either in prison, getting married or dying, so I started hanging out with my Sharon's younger friends. Then all of a sudden they started growing up too and that's when I knew I had to get out.

I had two choices; I either got myself a pair of bollocks and moved to London or I could kill myself. I didn't want to kill myself so I took the leap.

One day I said to my mum out of the blue, 'I'm going out for the day.' She said, 'What time will you be back?' I said I wasn't sure. I didn't go back for six months.

I got *Loot*, which was a London listings newspaper, and I went for a job in a bar called Cooper's in Waterloo station. I got the job there and then and I was so happy. I headed straight into Soho and went for a pint in a place called Barcode to celebrate. I had £35 in my pocket and I was scanning *Loot* for someone to live.

Back then, you could get a room in London for £50 a

week, but everywhere wanted a month's rent in advance and there was no way I'd be able to get my hands on that kind of money. I was basically fucked but the last thing I wanted to do was go back to Sittingbourne.

I was looking miserably into my drink when I heard this voice say, 'Stephen!' It turned out to be this Brazilian guy I'd pulled a few weeks earlier. I told him I was looking for somewhere to stay and he replied, 'Why don't you come and stay with me?'

CHRIS

The stars were aligned.

STEPHEN

They bloody were. I moved in with him in Clapham South and stayed there for six weeks while I worked at the bar and saved enough money for a deposit for a room. Then I moved into a flatshare in Finsbury Park that cost me £52 a week.

In some ways I felt like I'd missed the boat because I was so late leaving home. I felt so old, even at 22, because a lot of the guys I met when I was out clubbing were still in their teens.

I think I left everything so late because I was scared of life. Even thought I was miserable living at home I was scared of the unknown and it felt safer to stay in a crap situation than look around for something better. But in the end, it turned out I was also fine on my own. I could make a roast dinner at 13, and my mum always made sure all us kids could cook and clean and iron so I got used to looking after myself really quickly.

CHRIS

If you're so good all that stuff how come I did all the cooking when we were together?

STEPHEN

Because I'm lazy? I burnt your wok and made a mess of your kitchen the first time I tried to make us dinner and you never let me do it again. I'm not saying I did it on purpose but I still make out to Daniel that I can't cook so he does it all.

By the time I went back to Sittingbourne to see my mum I'd completely transformed. I had bleached blonde hair with two red spikes. I was wearing green velour trousers and black fuck-me Buffalo boots. I walked into my old estate looking like that, not giving a shit. Once I was out to myself I didn't give a fuck, even though I didn't come out to everyone else for another year. I marched down the high street looking like Dick Emery and when I arrived at my mum's she opened the door and went, 'Oh, fuck me.' She must have had some idea about my sexuality at that point, but I think she just thought I'd gone all 'London'.

I'd go and visit every three months or so and I deliberately had different-coloured hair every time. I'd been repressed for so long and now I had all the mad clothes I'd ever wanted. I just wore them all at the same time.

CHRIS

I think once you feel comfortable in yourself you feel like you have no boundaries.

STEPHEN

I did go a bit mad and bought loads of stuff I could never dream of wearing back in Kent. I loved my Buffalo boots. They were £80, but the kids' ones were half price so I bought them in a five. I'm a seven. I couldn't wear them that often because they squashed my feet so badly. My toes were like claws but they looked amazing.

CHRIS

I had an amazing pair of blue and white Buffalo boots. I loved them.

STEPHEN

I loved the freedom of wearing whatever I wanted. You can be so anonymous in London and no one gives a shit. I definitely went over the top sometimes but I wanted to try out everything and see what I liked most.

I feel the same way about Brighton. In a way we're in a

bubble because it's so accepting and no one bats an eyelid at anything. Sometimes we forget that it's not like that everywhere.

CHRIS

We are so lucky. I think we live in the best place on Earth and I don't think twice about holding hands with Tony when we're out. But if I went somewhere different I would be very aware of what I was doing because not everyone is open-minded.

STEPHEN

I didn't really stay in contact with anyone from Sittingbourne when I moved to London. I made new friends and all the people I met in London moulded me into the person I am today. I didn't really know who I was or have much guidance when I was a kid, but when I moved to London I met people from different backgrounds who had experienced so much and they influenced me hugely.

I had no idea I wanted to be a hairdresser until I was 23, but after working in loads of bars in London I wanted to do something that could be a career rather than just a job. I saw a sign in a salon called Headjogs in Bloomsbury saying they were looking for people for apprenticeships, but I didn't have the balls to go in and ask about it.

Eventually, after mulling it over for a few days, I walked in. I spoke to this lady called Shelley and we got on so well that she gave me a job on the spot. I swept the floor and washed hair for three years, but Shelley got me through my NVQ (which stands for Not Very Qualified).

I made two really good friends there called Madeline and Helen. Madeline was this little German girl and she was an amazing hairdresser and she really taught me the tricks of the trade, and we're still friends now. Helen was this really funny Essex girl and we ended up having a bit of a fling. We were having sex and she looked at me and said, 'Come on, you can do better than that.'

I'll always be grateful to Shelley for giving me my first break but I must admit that as soon as I got my NVQ I applied for a job at Toni and Guy, which was the place to work back then. I lied in my interview and told them I'd been working as a hairdresser for five years. I made up the names of salons I'd worked in down in Kent, and thankfully no one bothered to check.

I had to prove to them I was up to the job by doing three haircuts on mates, and as a result they gave me a twelve-week vardering (which is basically an intensive training programme) where I practised the ten basic Toni and Guy haircuts. If you could do those haircuts flawlessly at the end of those twelve weeks they'd give you a job.

There were 21 people in my class and I managed to pull the hottest bloke there. He was a six-foot Essex boy called Adrian and he had an alter ego called Amber, who was a real tart with a heart. I don't know what it is with me and men who like to dress up as women? He was living in Dalston and one evening he invited me over. I cycled for 40 minutes, but when I got there he bloody dumped me.

Only seven of us got a job, and it was bloody hard once I started working in a salon. But I didn't mind because I thought I'd made it, and they taught me to be a really good hairdresser.

While I did my training I worked behind the bar at a lesbian café called First Out, opposite Centre Point at the top of Oxford Street. I met a friend for life while I was working there. Carey and I have been through thick and thin. She was really unwell a couple of years ago and it really shook me up thinking I might lose her, but she pulled through. I call her 'Carey Jackson' after Michael Jackson because she's not a very good dancer. At my fortieth birthday party, Denise thought she was doing some kind of funny dance so she started copying her, and then realized she was being serious.

I was seeing this guy called Sam from the café and one day we went back to his flat in London Bridge. He introduced me to his flatmate Pete, and I was like, 'Ding dong. I want a bit of that.' Sam and I went to bed and halfway through the night I got up to go to the toilet. On the way back I looked at Sam's bedroom door and then looked at Pete's bedroom door and I thought, 'Hello'. I walked into Pete's bedroom and he said, 'About time!' We both knew there was something between us.

I woke up next to Pete in the morning and thought, 'Oh shit'. I crept back into Sam's room and he was still asleep so I started putting my clothes on. Suddenly I heard the sound of a duvet rustling and Sam growled, 'You slag,' at me.

After that, I started dating Pete and it broke Sam's heart. He would come home from work and Pete and I would be cuddled up on the sofa. How out of order is that?

CHRIS

That's a terrible story. Poor Sam. I hope you still feel guilty.

STEPHEN

I met a girl called Becky who started working at First Out just as I was leaving and we were inseparable for years. We used to encourage each other to be really naughty, and then we started sleeping with each other. Our friends used to say to us, 'You must be bisexual then?' and we'd be like, 'No, we're not. We're gay.'

We used to go to gay bars and do karaoke and we always sang 'California Dreamin' by The Mamas & the Papas. She had a great voice. She was also an actress and a voiceover artist. She was the voice of the Piccadilly Line. And I think maybe Thames Water.

We had this really intense friendship and then somehow we lost touch, but she got back in touch about a year ago and she's still as funny.

The first place I really felt settled in London was when I

moved in with a girl called Melissa in Brixton. We met on a night out and she was wearing this Sergio Tacchini tracksuit and a ponytail but she was incredibly posh. We got on really well and I loved living with her. Before that I'd been moving constantly and I never properly settled.

From 23 to 28 I was so promiscuous. And I had the time of my life. I was a cute boy back then. I had my pick of the lads and I made the most of it. I think I was trying to make up for all those lost 'straight' years.

I was out clubbing all the time and I *loved* it. I remember dancing away at Trade in Clerkenwell and I asked someone what time is was. They said it was 8.50am and I had to be at work in Wimbledon at 9am. I had to fly down there, make an excuse for being late and then do a day's work.

CHRIS

I ended working for Toni and Guy as well, as predicted by Betty. Rachel, who had trained me at Profile, left to go and work at Toni and Guy in High Wycombe, and her boss headhunted me shortly afterwards. I went straight to London for six weeks of training. It was such an amazing opportunity. I was terrified but everyone was lovely to me and I ended up getting a job in back at the High Wycombe branch.

After a year of working at Toni and Guy I met a guy called Greg in a bar and I was instantly attracted to him. After that we kept bumping into each other in different places and I just knew we were supposed to be together.

141

I fancied him so much. But then one night he said to me, 'You should go to Limelight tonight. It's lesbian night.' I was really confused until the penny finally dropped – he thought I was a bloody lesbian! To be fair it was during the time when I had the copper hair and the full-blown make-up so I was basically dressing as a girl. But I was still mortified. As was he, when I said I was a boy.

I kept seeing Greg all the time and I'd flirt with him like mad but he wasn't falling for my charms. One night I asked my friend Gary where he thought I was going wrong. Gary didn't mince his words and he said to me, 'You're *confusing*. You're a guy but you look like a girl. Straight men are going to be attracted to you because you look pretty, but you're a guy so they won't be interested. And gay guys aren't going to go for you because you look like a girl. You need to sort it out, love. Ditch the hair and the make-up and be a boy. Or have your willy cut off and become a girl. You can't have it all.'

After Gary gave me that pep talk I stopped wearing make-up and I cut my hair really short and bleached it blonde. I was in a bar called Comptons one night and Greg walked in. When he saw me he said, 'Oh my God, you're fucking gorgeous. You looked like a bird before but you're so *hot*.' We ended up snogging that night.

It took me a year to get Greg but I was with him for the next five and a half years and I was really happy. But in the end it all came too young and it was too soon for me to settle down. We bought a house together in Chesham and he even bought me a cat. It was all very grown up and settled, and I felt like I hadn't experienced enough. I'd only had a few snogs and Greg was the only man I'd ever slept with.

I was 26 and I hadn't been with anyone else. I still needed to explore a lot of things. Up until my early 20s I was still considering transitioning but I was too scared to go that extra step. Then the next thing I knew I was in this grown-up relationship and I just couldn't imagine myself staying that way forever.

STEPHEN

You did say to me once that if you could go back and have your time again you would have transitioned at 16 like you originally wanted to. Do you still feel like that?

CHRIS

In some ways I do, but back then it was *so* different. It wasn't talked about by anyone. And I started to lose my hair so all I kept thinking was, 'If I have a sex change I'm going to be a bald woman'. I didn't know that if I'd been given the right hormones I would never have lost my hair. My life could have been so different if we'd had the internet back then.

I do think even now we massively stereotype kids by assuming boys will be into football and the colour blue, and girls will be into dolls and pink things. Back in the olden days children were brought up wearing exactly the same clothes until the age of seven, so they all wore dresses. At the end of the day, anyone should be able to wear whatever they want.

I've seen a few guys walking around Brighton in what are classed as 'women's' clothes. But who says skirts are just for women? Where's the harm in a man wearing a skirt? It's shocking that there was a time when women weren't allowed to wear trousers, but to a certain extent we're still in a time where men can't wear skirts.

STEPHEN

I quite like a man in a skirt. Look at kilts. They're so sexy. Remember when we went to Glasgow together for a work thing and our aim was to try and find out what really goes on underneath a kilt? We'd only been there for about five minutes when we spotted a guy wearing a lovely blue one and he was really happy for us to pop our hands up. He loved it but his wife was getting a bit pissed off. Mind you, we were feeling up her husband, so fair enough, really.

Will Young's started wearing dresses now and he looks great. And this guy we know has got a son of five and he often comes downstairs wearing his sister's clothes with make-up on. He says to his dad, 'Do I look pretty?' His dad says to him, 'You look *beautiful*,' and that's how it should be. I think it's brilliant that his dad is embracing it.

CHRIS

I always say there are 'men' and there are 'women' and there are so many different degrees in between. When I was a little boy my neighbour had the best dressing-up box on the estate. It had this pink dress with black polka dots on it and I loved it so much. As a boy who was curious about being a girl it was a dream come true, but I was never allowed to wear it.

One day the other kids said I could try it on and it was like all my Christmases had come at once. I was dancing and twirling around the garden and I felt so pretty. Then my bubble was burst when my friend's mum shouted over the fence to my mum, 'Oi, Doreen. Come and sort your fucking son out. He's prancing around in a *dress*.' I felt so humiliated. But I looked *lovely*.

My older sister Marie went really gothy when she was at college and I had really long hair that was dyed black at the time. She wanted to make me look like Robert Smith from The Cure so she backcombed my hair and put loads of make-up on me. I was probably about 14 and I had loads of eyeliner and red lipstick on, and of course I thought it was great. When I walked into the kitchen my dad looked at me and shook his head in disgust and walked out into the garden. I'll never shake that off.

STEPHEN

I think when people used to think about people being gay they just thought about the sex element of it. And the campness and all that. Being gay was almost a cliché when we were young.

I remember going into C&A with my mum when I was about 13 and I found this top. It was hideous. It was luminous orange with luminous yellow shoulders and luminous green stripes going through it. I was like a gym top or something and I told my mum I wanted it and she said, 'It's a fucking girls' top!' But I begged her to buy it for me and I wore it non-stop.

Back then I used to blow-dry my hair like Lady Di's and I put so much hairspray in it when the wind blew my entire (massive) fringe used to lift up. How the hell can people not have realized?

CHRIS

When I got bored of having my hair black I dyed it a proper peroxide blonde. I used to put Once liquid mousse in, scrunch it and leave it. As the day went on it would go dryer and dryer, but I was still the envy of my schoolmates because I had these amazing blonde curls.

I decided I was sick of scrunching it all the time because it took so long, so my mate Maria and I got a home perming kit so I could just wash it and leave it. We put my hair in foam curlers and then applied the solution. When we rinsed it off the roots were really, really curly and the rest of it was almost straight. Thankfully it was such a cheap box job it only lasted about two days.

LIVE AND LET DYE

STEPHEN

Considering we're both hairdressers we've had our fair share of bad hairstyles over the years.

CHRIS

Christ, I know. The first year I went to the Toni and Guy Awards I was 19 and I had my hair bleached up and it went a bit wrong. My boss said I couldn't go to the awards with pale yellow hair so he suggested I dye it purple. When he washed the colour off it was the brightest cerise pink you've ever seen.

STEPHEN

I bet you looked like Mrs Slocombe. 'Has anyone seen my pussy?'

CHRIS

It didn't even look *that* good. It wasn't a cool colour. It was luminous. I dyed it at the end of the day on a Friday and the awards were the following evening. I was working all day so there was no time to do anything about it. My mum was horrified when I got home. I went into work the following day in black PVC trousers, a black vest and platforms with this cerise pink hair. I was waiting at the bus stop and people were almost crashing their cars when they drove past.

When I arrived at the awards there was another girl there with bright pink hair and everyone kept saying we were hair twins. Hers looked terrible too. I was mortified. I had a bleach bath on my hair at work on the Monday and after about two minutes the pink came out and it went white blonde and it was such a relief. But I did think, 'Fucking hell. We could have done that on Friday and saved me a lot of humiliation.'

STEPHEN

I dyed my hair every colour going, just because I could. It was bright blue once and I was on the tube going to work. We stopped at Green Park and this bloke who was standing with a big group of lads shouted '*Blue* Park' and everyone sniggered. I felt like such a cock.

CHRIS

I had my hair peroxide blonde for many, many years and I grew it into a mohican. I always dyed the longer back bit a shade called 'juicy mandarin'. It was a bright orange colour and when I got bored of that I dyed it baby pink. But – and yes, I am about to say this – I thought it looked too gay.

STEPHEN

I did some pretty awful haircuts on people back in the early days while I was still training. People could come in and get their hair done really cheaply, or even for free, but in return they had to kind of let us do what we wanted.

One day this woman with really curly ginger hair came in and showed me a photo of a girl with really short hair and a long fringe and said she wanted hers to look just like that. These days I'd tell her there's no way it would work, but she was insistent and I was naïve.

I started off by cutting the sides and back off, and then I started shaping the fringe. At one point I looked up and she was eyeballing me in the mirror like she hated me. To be fair, her hair was still wet and she looked like fucking Mick Hucknall. And it wasn't about to get any better.

I straightened the front and started cutting into it, desperately trying to make it look like it was in some kind of style. When I'd finished I took a step back, smiled and said, 'How's that? It's what you wanted, isn't it?'

Her eyes welled up and she kept trying to pull her fringe down. All I kept thinking was that the minute she got home and washed it was going to go curly again and she'd end up looking like she was wearing one of those wigs you see advertised in the back of Sunday supplements.

CHRIS

One of my biggest hairdressing disasters was when I did my sister Sharon's highlights for her before I'd done any proper training. She didn't want to pay to go and get them done and I was *convinced* I could do a good job.

She had really long, thick, dark, curly hair and I remember pulling sections of it through one of those old fashioned plastic caps. I bleached the hell out of it and I felt really pleased with myself because the colour had taken. But as I pulled the cap off all the blonde bits snapped off so she had these wispy little tufts sticking out of the top of her head and no highlights. I was crying laughing but she was furious with me and it took her ages to grow the stumpy bits out.

Poor Shazza didn't have a lot of luck with her hair. Another time, when she was about 14, she wanted a bob. I told her not to do it because even at that tender age I knew it would look shit because of her curls, but you could never tell her what to do.

One day she came home with all her hair cut just below her ears and it looked like a frizzy triangle. Marie went mad and told her she needed to cut it properly to even it out. Marie didn't know a thing about cutting hair but she kept hacking at it until there was almost nothing left. By the time she stopped snipping poor Sharon looked like she was wearing a curly toupee.

Sharon was crying her eyes out and she refused to go to school, so my mum had to get a home hairdresser round to sort it out. She ended up with this really cool short, edgy style. At least I thought it was cool. Sharon cried her eyes out again because she thought she looked like a boy.

STEPHEN

That poor girl. I think I would have cried too. Someone said to me the other day that your hairdressing clientele is a reflection of you, and I seem to get a lot of chatty women in the salon. I'm sure some clients see it as a bit

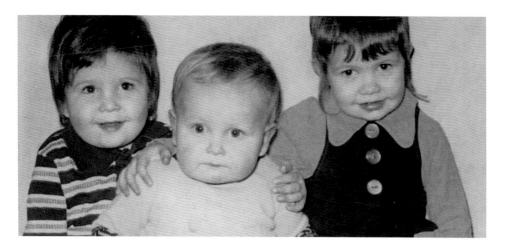

Top: Me, Paul and Denise. Those haircuts were trendy at the time.

Left: All the Webbs, 1976. Mum rocking the Farrah Fawcett look.

Bottom: Me, Denise and Paul in Christmas hats. Mum dressed me and Paul identically – we both look really happy about it.

Left: Paul, me and my nan: the matriarch. We all adored her.

Below: Me and Paul visiting my dad in Holland for the first time, and looking pretty excited!

Below left: Me in my school uniform – I was the only boy in my class with a pierced ear. What a badass.

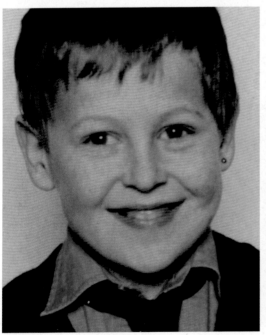

Top left: Me in a particularly snazzy woollen waistcoat. That wallpaper was at home, even though it looks like a dodgy pub.

Above: Giving my sister Beverly away: one of my proudest moments.

Left: Me and Mummy Pat. Before my sister's wedding, drinking champagne in the garden. Lovely day.

Top: Me and Daniel with our beautiful god-daughter Sia Willow.

Left: Me and Daniel at the Taj Mahal, just after getting engaged!

Above left: Me aged 3. The first and only time I've ever been angelic.

Above: Me, dad and my sister Sharon. One of his rare breaks from digging graves.

Left: The whole family together. I must have been about 7. Check out the groovy wallpaper and my sisters' clothes!

Above: Me, Marie and my dodgy fringe.

Above right: Me, Sharon and her dodgy fringe. Thanks Mum – queen of the bad haircuts.

Right: I'm about 12 here. The only childhood photo of me with good hair.

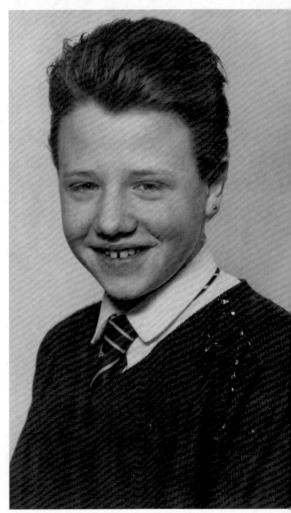

Top left: Me and my friend at 17. Post-school, pre-hairdressing.

Above: Christina. Check out her legs!

Centre left: The photo that captured Stephen and Tony's hearts. Who can blame them?

Left: One of my favourite pictures with me and Ginge. Taken before he died – obviously.

Above: Me and my lovely mum. You can see where I got my good looks from.

Right: One of my happiest days – when Tony made an honest man of me. He took me up the Eiffel!

Below: Tony and I meeting Rusty and Buddy for the first time. It was love at first sight.

of a therapy session. I love it because I get to sit there and chat for hours on end, and you can get such an insight into people's lives.

CHRIS

People tell me all sorts when I'm doing their hair. I've had women telling me about their affairs and marriage break-ups – all sorts. I think they really trust me and feel like they can open up.

I have some really funny clients as well. One lady was telling me about her mate who sells Christmas trees and she said to me, 'He makes an absolute killing. Every year he makes around £80,000 in a month. I mean, if he did that a couple of times a year he'd be laughing.'

STEPHEN

She's got a point.

CHRIS

You can literally change someone's life by doing their hair. I suggested to one client of mine that she went blonde because I thought it would really suit her. She went for it and it gave her a massive confidence boost. She started going to the gym, met a guy when they sat next to each other on the exercise bikes and moved in with him. All that from just a change of colour. I don't think her husband was that thrilled, mind you.

STEPHEN

You should start pimping yourself out as a hairdresser-slash-life coach.

CHRIS

I think on the whole, people tend to play it safer with their hair as they get older. It's the same for most things, isn't it?

STEPHEN

I wish I'd played it safe with tattoos when I was younger. I got my first tattoo when I was 16. I had it done at this tattoo parlour in Rochester in Kent, and I only chose that place because the guy who worked there was renowned for not asking for ID. You had to be either 18 or have your parents' permission to get one done, and there was no way my mum was going to give me her blessing.

This was back when tattoo shops had all the pictures of tattoos on the wall and you had to ask for a certain number. I looked at them all and pointed to a shit panther and said, 'I'll have number 17 on my arm.' Weirdly, Chris, you did exactly the same thing, didn't you?

CHRIS

I did, so we both had shit panthers! I also got mine when I was 16. My sister Marie was 18 so I took her with me. The tattooist said to me, 'Are you old enough to get this done?' and I replied, 'Yeah, I'm 18 and I've bought my older sister with me to prove it.' That was probably the worst validation *ever.*

I couldn't afford the first tattoo I chose because it was £30 so I chose 16B instead, and I was stuck with this terrible panther's head for the next 20 years until I got it covered up.

STEPHEN

Loads of guys of about 30 or 40 were having those kinds of tattoos back then and they're not fashionable anymore, so you only really see them on 65-year-old men. And Chris and I. Mine has lasted pretty well and I had the outline redone in 2008. I decided I wanted to add to it so I had a load of sailor tattoos like Lady Luck and cards, cherries, dice and a heart put around it.

CHRIS

You're so lucky you've still got a lot of the detail on your panther because so many of them look smudged and shit. I had my second tattoo when I was about 20. It was a black dragon with claws that looked like it was scratching my back. Ten years later it had faded so much it looked like a black dribble.

STEPHEN

I must admit, I started having tattoos because as a kid I wanted people to look at me.

CHRIS

Did you want people to think you were hard?

STEPHEN

I just wanted to be different and back then everyone wasn't covered in tattoos like they are now.

CHRIS

It's the norm now. The funny thing is that in 40 years all these old ladies aren't going to be wearing twin sets and pearls; they'll all be covered in big tattoos.

STEPHEN

I was at the beach in the summer and all these blokes were walking past covered in tattoos and I thought it looked rancid. They all had big beer bellies and tons of tats. That's what I think I look like. That's why I'm getting all of my mine lazered off. It cost me hundreds to have them put on and it's going to cost me thousands, and a lot of pain, to get them off again.

CHRIS

Having a tattoo removed definitely hurts more than having a tattoo done. I had the dragon taken off my back and a rose put in its place and it was agony.

LIVE AND LET DYE

STEPHEN

If I could click my fingers and get rid of all my tattoos now and replace them with intricate, delicate modern ones I would. A lot of modern tattoos are beautiful but mine are all thick and heavy.

CHRIS

Tattoo trends have changed so much. When I started having my cover-ups four years ago, no guys had flowers or butterflies. I didn't want the Aztec tattoos everyone was getting then, but now everyone's got ones like mine.

STEPHEN

I'm so glad I didn't have a Celtic band around my arm. They look terrible now. They're so old-fashioned.

When I was in my twenties I was covered in tattoos and piercings and I thought I looked the bollocks, and when I see young kids now with the same they look great. But you get older and you change. You grow up.

CHRIS

Tattoos don't look good on all young kids. The guys in One Direction have got really shit tattoos, in my opinion.

STEPHEN

I think they look like prison tattoos, but they're 'in' aren't they? And I don't fancy Harry Styles like the rest of the world.

CHRIS

I can honestly say I don't give a shit what One Direction do now they've split up. I have no interest in them whatsoever. And I find that whole Liam and Cheryl thing weird. I'm sorry, but it is. And that tattoo of hers on her arse. . . When do you think it's taking things too far with tattoos?

STEPHEN

Face.

CHRIS

Or neck? I've got one at the back of my neck and you can slightly see it if I'm wearing a smart shirt, but I don't want to look like Jeremy McConnell from *Celebrity Big Brother*. I think his look shit, and they are all green, which is the most difficult colour to remove.

As well as tons of tattoos I'm sick of blokes having massive bushy beards, even though I've got one. But mine is neat. I think a lot of guys are using them to improve their look. As soon as they get a beard they can go from a one out of ten to an eight out of ten.

STEPHEN

That's true. When beards go out of fashion a lot of people are going to realize they've been dating ugly blokes.

CHRIS

Blokes who have got no chins are going to be exposed too. They probably all look like Gail Tilsley underneath that fuzz.

STEPHEN

I can't grow a beard. I can just about grow a George Michael goatee, but that's it. I've got quite a hairless face.

CHRIS

What do you think will be the next big trend? Do you think curtains will come back?

STEPHEN

People have said that. Imagine? I could be fashionable again. Mullets came back so why not curtains?

CHRIS

Do you think Billy Ray Cyrus mullets will ever be a thing? There was a Spanish guy at my gym recently who had a full-on mullet and it looked alright. Not great but *alright*.

STEPHEN

I like it when women have their heads shaved and then have it long at the front. I think it looks great.

CHRIS

I'm bored of teenage girls walking around with pink and purple hair now. I did that years ago.

STEPHEN

And the woodchopper look in general is a bit done for men now.

CHRIS

It's called a 'lumbersexual' and I think it's lovely. I think they look really sexy with their checked shirts.

STEPHEN

I like men wearing plimsolls and socks. That's the new thing.

CHRIS

And I like trousers that look like they've shrunk in the wash a bit.

STEPHEN

I saw a bloke wearing three-quarter-length trousers the other day and that didn't look good. That was too nineties.

CHRIS

Shrinkage to just above the ankle is cool, but if it's too high you look like a dick.

LIVE AND LET DYE

STEPHEN

I think to wear anything like that you have to be slim and young. You can't be a fat old bloke squeezing yourself into hipster jeans. Whatever fashion is in I can take a bit of inspiration from it as a 45-year-old man, but I wouldn't go crazy.

CHRIS

You always need to tone it down. You don't want to look like mutton dressed as lamb. There was a point when I was younger when I promised myself I would never be that, but now I feel like I'm on the cusp. If I'm not careful I could end up looking a bit tragic.

I buy some things I love on the spur of the moment and then when I get them home and try them on I think, 'Oh no'. I know I have to take them back because I look like a twat.

STEPHEN

I'm much more careful with fashion now. I stick to black, grey, blue and green.

CHRIS

Colours that are slimming, basically?

STEPHEN

Basically. I bought a peach-coloured outfit a few months ago and when I put it on I look like a right dickhead. The only way I can ever wear it is if I decide to go to the south of France on holiday. And lose weight. I'm better in plain clothes. You can only get away with outrageous shirts if you're very slim. And I'm not. I need to go on a proper diet.

CHRIS

You're so all or nothing though. It was only six months ago you were going to the gym five times a week.

STEPHEN

I know. I just find it hard. I love a kebab after a night out. And I did put on weight when I was living with my mum. She's got no concept of portion sizes and I'm greedy so she'd get a big lemon cheesecake and cut it in half and we'd eat it between us. Then an hour later we'd have a cup of tea and an éclair.

CHRIS

I used to go to the gym all the time, BS – Before Stephen – and I had the most amazing body. He was the one who got me out of the habit of working out. I thought, 'If he can't be bothered to stay in shape then neither can I'. He wasn't making any effort at all. I'd done two years of really healthy eating and going to the gym and all of a sudden I started dating Stephen and I got fat.

160

STEPHEN

I don't know what it is with food. I can make a massive shepherd's pie and just have a quarter of it. Then I'll go back and have another quarter. Then two hours later I can go and eat the other half. I'm like a bottomless pit.

CHRIS

You should go and get yourself one of those. . .

STEPHEN

Fitbits?

CHRIS

Gastric bands.

STEPHEN

They wouldn't give me one. Believe it or not I'm not fat enough. And once you've had one you spend the rest of your life only being able to eat one spoonful of yoghurt and you're full up. I'd never be able to eat a Sunday dinner again.

CHRIS

That's not true. A friend of mine has one and she can still eat quite a lot, but certain foods like chicken and pasta bloat her. She still goes out for dinner and has a good meal.

STEPHEN

Even if I went privately I don't think they'd do it. I have got to lose some weight though. I can't remember the last time I felt starving hungry because I'm always picking. And boozing is terrible for your weight.

CHRIS

You hear about these young girls who are trying to lose weight and they'll save up all their calories and drink wine instead of eating. I think that's terrible. It's so unhealthy.

STEPHEN

My mate's a trolley dolly and he was saying that he had a very famous woman on his flight recently and she only had one mint tea in twelve hours. One mint tea! That's how you stay slim.

CHRIS

It always makes me laugh when people go into McDonalds and order ten large Big Mac meals and then ask for a Diet Coke. The thing with me is that I don't like feeling full. I would rather feel starving hungry than feel really stuffed.

STEPHEN

Oooh, no. I'd much rather be stuffed full. When I'm in the zone I can be really good with health and fitness, but I'm very easily distracted. When I was with Chris I did this diet where I only ate things that were white, like egg whites and chicken.

CHRIS

Then during the second week he went up a level and went to a different colour. Was it orange? It was something ridiculous like that.

STEPHEN

I ate a lot of carrots. We went on this trip to Leeds Castle together and there was all this amazing food laid out for us and I didn't eat any of it. I was so miserable.

CHRIS

That's the thing – when you're on a diet you're a miserable bastard.

STEPHEN

I am much more fun when I let myself go.

CHRIS

Then you're just mildly annoying.

STEPHEN

I've had personal trainers and I get well into it and then I fall off the wagon again. I wish someone would send me to a boot camp for three months somewhere lovely where I'm locked away and all my meals are prepared for me and I'm barked at to do exercise every morning. Then I'll come back and loads of my friends would be waiting for me in a bar. I'd turn up looking all slim and beautiful and they'd all gasp.

CHRIS

If I ever won the lottery the first two things I'd do would be to get myself a chef and a personal trainer. I'd have someone cooking all my meals and making me work out.

STEPHEN

I'm really tempted to go and get some liposuction. I've had it before. I went to Belgium to get it done because it's so cheap. Even though I was a lot slimmer back then they managed to take out a litre of fat. I also had my top and bottom bags removed from my eyes while I was out cold. In for a penny.

I had to wear a crotchless corset for six weeks to hold everything in place. I went to stay with my sister in Holland for a week and then I flew straight to India for six months. I wore the corset for two days but it was bloody boiling so I binned it. Despite that I still had a flat belly for the first time in years.

CHRIS

Didn't you have all of that done because one of your friends that you hadn't seen for ages told you that you looked like shit?

STEPHEN

Yeah, but I was contemplating getting my eyes done anyway because I didn't wear glasses back then and I always looked tired. Every time I saw friends they'd say, 'Ooh, were you out last night?' And I hadn't been. So I just went for it. They've bagged a bit again now but I'm still glad I had it done.

Apparently, after they put me under, just as the surgeon was getting everything prepared, he turned on the radio and Chicago's 'If You Leave Me Now' was playing. I started singing and clicking my fingers along to it and he said he'd never experienced anything like it before. He told me I had to lie still, and with that I put my arms down and I was out cold again.

The next thing I remember was coming to with a nurse each side of me trying to squeeze me into this crotchless corset. I was off my head on the painkillers so I was laughing my head off. Then I looked down at my willy and said to them both, 'You wouldn't think something so small could get you into so much trouble.'

They put me in a recovery room and gave me a cup of tea and a biscuit and I felt like I'd never eaten before. It was gorgeous. It was almost worth the pain just for that moment.

CHRIS

Obviously I haven't had anything like done because I'm one hundred percent natural. Apart from my teeth. My spray tans. Botox. And three hair transplants.

I got the hair transplants because when I was young my dad was really bald. He had just a few sparse hairs on top but it was all thick and curly around the sides. I remember looking at him and thinking, 'I love my dad, but I don't want hair like that'. And I knew if I carried on the way I was going I'd end up as bald as a coot.

My hair started receding when I was 18 and I panicked. I covered it up for years and I even started wearing wigs and toupees at one point. I have to say, they did look amazing, but they were causing so much damage to my scalp I knew it wasn't a long-term solution.

I booked myself in for a hair transplant the day after my thirty-fifth birthday. I always said I didn't want to be a 35-year-old bald, camp hairdresser. So at least I was only a 35-year-old bald, camp hairdresser for one day.

That was five years ago and although it worked well, I wanted another one. My crown was really thinning and I remember finding out that Callum Best had had three hair transplants done by this guy called Dr Asim Shahmalak at the Crown Clinic. I knew I had to go to him.

I went for a consultation and we got on so well. He's a right character. I was impressed with him and his team of people and all the aftercare they offered. We've got a long-term plan.

LIVE AND LET DYE

The second time I had a transplant Dr Shahmalak thickened it and filled in some bits and it was such a big confidence booster. When someone turns around and says, 'Oh my God, your hair looks really good,' it makes me so happy. And having hair does make you feel younger. It's a simple fact that balding men seem older than guys with a full head of hair.

STEPHEN

It looks so much better now you've got no dye on it. When you had it really dark it looked like you were trying to disguise the fact you were going bald. Now you just look like you've got. . . hair.

CHRIS

Because it was so fine before I thought that by having it dark I could disguise it, but it looked fake. I was also having to dye it every two weeks because I'm so grey.

They had to shave my head for my hair transplant in January because I had what's known as an FUE transplant. I knew I wouldn't be able to colour it for about five months so I let it go grey and as it's grown out I've started to really like it.

But that doesn't mean I'm going to stop dying my beard because that is a bit iffy when it's natural. I've got a bright ginger moustache and two white clusters that look like I've got a couple of tarantulas trying to escape from my chin.

Then it's salt and pepper everywhere else and it doesn't matter how short it is, it looks messy.

I've toned down my fake tan now and I'm not as orange as I used to be, so I am genuinely going for a bit more of a natural look. But the beard dye is here to stay.

STEPHEN

Would you have any other work done in the future?

CHRIS

I have considered getting liposuction on my tummy because I've got a little paunch that won't go away no matter how much I work out.

STEPHEN

I reckon if you had it done you'd see your six-pack because you are quite muscly. You've got good pecs. I need a bra for mine.

CHRIS

At one point when we were together we did look at your stomach and it looked like Homer Simpson.

STEPHEN

It did. My tits were his eyes and then my stomach was his mouth going 'Doh'. But I think if you want to have a tweak of something and you've got the money, why not?

CHRIS

Definitely, but I do think you should take time to research and maybe live with your decision for a little while and then make sure you still want to go ahead. In my early twenties I had a really big nose and I was so thin that I looked like Meg the Witch. I got myself a £5,000 loan so I could get a nose job, but then when I went for the consultation they wanted £6,500. All I could think was, 'I've got to find another £1,500 to get this bloody thing off my face'. In the end I totally bottled it, and I'm glad I did.

STEPHEN

Your nose is *you*.

CHRIS

I've grown into it because I've bulked up a bit, so if I had a little diddy nose now it would look weird on me. At least my big conk suits me as I am. So I would say don't rush into anything because your attitude may change.

STEPHEN

I don't think people should do anything until they're well into their thirties. It doesn't matter if you've got a big nose or you think you've got bags under your eyes, there aren't really any ugly 16-year-olds. Their skin is great and you don't find many teenagers that have fallen out of the ugly tree and hit every branch on the way down.

CHRIS

Yet they probably do think they're ugly. So many teenagers have issues. These days we constantly have photos of beautiful people in front of us telling us how we should look. And selfies are a nightmare. People get obsessed with making them perfect. To the point where they don't even look like themselves anymore.

STEPHEN

Everywhere does Botox now. It's the norm to get it at your dentist.

CHRIS

The thing is, once you have the thing you're most insecure about fixed you'll look for something else. Especially when you're young. I *hated* my teeth and when I was 16 I heard about this NHS dentist who everyone said was brilliant. He looked like a seventies porn star with these long flowing locks and a hairy chest. I told him how much I hated my teeth and said that I always put my hand in front of my mouth in photos, and he said I could get them capped on the NHS.

The thing is, with veneers, you need to get them redone about every 15 years and I could have done with getting mine done in my early thirties. Then my gums started receding and I had my front four teeth replaced in my late thirties.

And as soon as I got my teeth done when I was 16, that was when I got obsessed with my nose. There will always be something.

STEPHEN

So many young people are getting Botox done as 'prevention'. You don't need it when you're 21. Jane Fonda's work is amazing. She's still got crow's feet and other lines, but she's had subtle work and she looks great.

CHRIS

Sharon Osbourne looked amazing at one point but now I think she's gone too far. It's the same with Kylie. She calmed down with the Botox, though, thankfully.

STEPHEN

And don't you think Madonna is looking as weird as Michael Jackson used to? Her transformation has happened over a long period of time but it must scare some kids. Her fillers are out of control I reckon. Some people look much better before surgery, which is sad, because it's hard to undo stuff once it's been done.

CHRIS

She needs to stop wearing see-through clothes. A woman of her age can still wear cool clothes but she does look like mutton dressed as lamb.

STEPHEN

And you don't want to see her boobs out all the time. They're going to be like socks with sand in them soon.

CHRIS

The best publicity stunt Madonna's ever pulled was when she fell backwards off those stairs at the BRITs last year.

STEPHEN

Do you think it definitely was a stunt? If it was then it was done in a very clever way because she was on the front page of every newspaper in the world. I've watched that clip so many times. It's bloody brilliant.

CHRIS

I think so, although I'm surprised she didn't break a hip at her age.

STEPHEN

Why doesn't Madonna just disappear and enjoy her life and her money and her children? She could go somewhere where she isn't recognized and have a really nice life. Why keep making a fool of yourself?

CHRIS

With the money she's got she could buy her own island and lie on a beach and get served cocktails by handsome men.

I don't want to sound ageist, but apart from Dolly Parton and Barbra Streisand, everyone should give up at a certain time.

Surgery can enhance someone's career, but it can also destroy it. Look at Jennifer Grey from *Dirty Dancing*. She didn't work again after she got her nose job. But James Nesbitt's career took off again after he had a hair transplant. And I heard that if it helps your career it's tax deductible. If a model is losing their hair and they have a hair transplant they can claim for it because they're having it to enhance their career.

I know some celebrities deny they've had any work done and it's so obvious. Why not just come out and say it?

STEPHEN

I don't know why people try to deny it. Victoria Beckham used to say she hadn't had a boob job. She wasn't fooling anyone.

Chapter Six

BRIGHTON ROCKS

Stephen: 'I got Chris an Easter egg and some cat food for Valentine's Day.'

STEPHEN

I stayed in London until I was 30 and I loved it. But I felt like I was getting stuck in a rut and I needed something new.

On my thirtieth birthday I found myself in King's Cross Hospital having my tonsils taken out. I thought I'd pop in at 2pm, have them whipped out and be home again by 5pm. But my bloody tonsils ruptured and I was in there for four days.

I didn't take any overnight stuff with me and I remember a nurse waking me up saying, 'Mr Webb, have you got any pyjamas?' I didn't even have a toothbrush. To make things worse, when I eventually properly came round from the anaesthetic I'd shit the bed. A nurse helped me to the shower room and gave me a bar of soap the size of a stamp to wash myself with. What the fuck was I supposed to do with that?

The hospital sorted me out some pyjamas and put me on a wing with a load of other people who had throat problems. Everyone was talking like they were using a vocoder. It was like sharing a room with 15 Cher impersonators. I had bugger all to do so I lay there reflecting on my life. I knew I couldn't keep partying forever and I'd never been travelling so I thought, 'Fuck it'.

Two weeks later I landed at Bombay airport with my friend Becky from First Out at 3am. I had about £2,000 in the bank to last me a year and I stood in the airport arrivals hall thinking, 'What have I done?' I hated it on sight.

I stayed in Bombay for about five days, hating it a little bit more each day. The poverty in India was such a shock and I didn't think it was something I'd ever get used to. Then suddenly something clicked and I fell in love with the place. I don't know what happened but I suppose I just acclimatized to everything and I felt settled. It also helped that I discovered you could buy Valium over the counter.

India was the start of a new phase for me. My twenties had been a right laugh but I wanted to grow up a bit and to get know myself better. I was bored of being constantly hungover and knackered and I wanted to learn and explore.

We headed to Goa and then on to Kerala but Becky and

I fell out so I travelled round on my own. I ended up working for the Missionaries of Charity in Calcutta, which was founded by Mother Teresa. That was a life-changing time for me. My first position was in a children's home, but when I found out that one of my jobs was untying the children from their beds each morning I couldn't stay. It was too upsetting. I'd be in charge of five children and I had to untie them, put them on a potty and spoon-feed them porridge. I'd play with them and make things as nice as I could but I found it heartbreaking.

I went back to the charity's office and told them how I felt and they totally understood. They sent me to work in a hospice instead, so I was looking after people who were dying. That was also incredibly difficult, but I found it easier looking after adults, and I stayed there for two weeks.

I spent six months in India, and I came back to the UK via a trip to Mount Everest. People had told me how incredible it was so I set myself a challenge to experience it.

I travelled to Kathmandu in Nepal, where I planned to join an organized trip. I couldn't find anything that was less than £2,000, and there was no way I could afford that. So I decided to hire a rucksack and sleeping bag. I bought about twelve tins of tuna and got a flight to this tiny airport called Lukla in north-eastern Nepal. I thought I'd get there and jump in a cab to the nearest town, but you literally land on the side of a mountain and there aren't any cars. You have to travel everywhere by yak.

I started walking up the mountain on my own but when I got to day five it got so steep I was absolutely exhausted. I was also quite breathless because there's 50 per cent less oxygen up there. I remember falling to my knees and contemplating going back, but it would have taken me five days to get back to the airport – the same amount of time it would take for me to get to Base Camp. I was already halfway there, so it seemed stupid to give up at that point.

This Nepalese guy came jogging past and asked if I needed help. He suggested we walked to the next village, which was a few miles away, and have a rest. You pass by lots of villages as you're trekking and you can knock on anyone's door and they'll usually let you stay for a fee. They'll also feed you, but it's usually a really watery broth with some bok choi in it, so there's not a lot of substance to it.

As you get higher nothing grows and the mountain's surface is made up of massive rock boulders. It's like being on another planet and the views are unbelievable. Also, the higher up you go the more expensive things are and you end up paying £3.50 for a Mars bar. But you need it because you crave a lot of sugar.

The lovely man carried my bag for me to the next village and the walk took us two hours. He said if he'd been on his own it would have taken him twenty minutes! He offered to stay with me until I got to Base Camp, but he said he'd only travel me with if I stopped smoking. Yes, I was still smoking despite the lack of oxygen and he did have a point.

You pass graves along the way from where people have got altitude sickness and died, and smoking definitely wasn't doing me any favours.

We got to Base Camp, and after giving myself a big pat on the back the man took me back to where he'd found me. From there I managed to find my way back to the airport. Although I use the term 'airport' loosely. It looks like a giant car park and when you take off the plane taxis to the end of the runway and literally falls off the side of the mountain. It's crazy.

When I got back to Kathmandu, because I'd been walking for so long with so little oxygen my respiratory system was really weak. I couldn't get out of bed for three days and I think that's when the exhaustion properly kicked in.

But I did it, and I got to Base Camp One and back for £450. I was insane to do it on my own and I wouldn't do it like that again, but I felt such a sense of achievement. I also went up weighing 13 stone and came down ten stone because I had so little to eat, which is always a nice bonus.

CHRIS

India and the Himalayas sound like incredible places, and they obviously had a massive effect on you.

STEPHEN

It did. It changed a lot for me. When I came back I started working for Mencap, because I'd been hairdressing for a long time and I felt like I wanted to do something that meant more. After seeing the conditions people were living in out in India I wanted to carry on helping people.

I looked after three autistic guys who were non-verbal and doubly incontinent, and they could be quite aggressive at times. But it was another amazing experience and it taught me a lot.

I worked for Mencap for two years but because it was a very demanding job I ended up getting really run down and quite ill. I also missed being creative, so when I was offered my job back at Toni and Guy I accepted.

My thirties ended up being a mixed time and some of it was great, and some of it was terrible.

CHRIS

My life really changed when I moved to Brighton when I was 26. I'd always had a real pull towards the city, ever since I'd visited it in my early twenties. After spending a weekend there with Paul I knew for sure I was ready to pack up and start again.

Sadly my relationship with Paul was coming to a natural end and I needed a fresh start. I walked into Toni and Guy in Brighton town centre and asked if they were looking for any staff. It was such a cool place and when they offered me a job I was over the bloody moon.

Mine and Paul's house in Chesham went on the market the following week and sold straight away, so I moved down to Brighton in December 2001. There's something about the freedom of Brighton that makes you feel like you can be anything you want to be, and achieve anything you want to achieve.

I made friends with people at the salon and I met loads of new people in bars and clubs, and I finally felt like I belonged somewhere. I had this newfound confidence and that's when I properly started really expressing myself and I dressed up as my alter ego Christina more and more.

I'd walk around all dressed up; people would say to me, 'Oh my God, you're *amazing*,' whereas in the past people would often think (and sometimes say), 'Oh my God, you're a *freak*.'

I remember being at Pride one year and I saw this pink checked rah-rah skirt I *loved*. My friend Jaime, who also used to dress up, said it was naff but I still bought it and I based my entire outfit around it that night. I was wearing pink legwarmers, a pink bikini top and white stilettoes, with this little skirt sitting in between. I curled my hair and put on really good make-up and I thought I looked amazing.

I'll never forget the first time I met Jaime. It was March 2002 and the first time I went to this club night called Wild Fruit in Brighton. She came over to me and said, 'You remind me of a younger version of my friend Jilly.' I was introduced to Jilly later in the evening and I said to her, 'Oh, Jaime just told me I look like a younger version of you.' She gave me a really steely look and stormed off, and it wasn't until I properly thought about it I realized that she may have taken it the wrong way. She clearly thought I was being bitchy but I honestly didn't mean anything by it. I don't always think before I speak.

I used to see Jilly out all the time after that and we did get on. She was always saying that I should hang out with her and her group of friends more, but she was still always slightly off with me. I don't think she ever quite forgave me for basically calling her old.

Jaime and I could easily get away with going to London for the day dressed as women, and no one would be any the wiser. We'd walk around Harrods and all these guys would tell me I was beautiful. This was around the time Chantelle Houghton won *Big Brother* and I used to get mistaken for her all the time. Looking back at photos of myself I can totally see why.

I loved the admiration I got from doing Christina. I remember walking into a pub with my hair all pinned up, wearing this fake-fur coat and high-heeled boots. This group of women said to me, 'You look so amazing. We love your outfit,' and I replied, 'This isn't my outfit. *This* is my outfit.' And with that I dropped my coat to the floor and I was standing there wearing white stockings and suspenders, white French knickers, a white bra and loads of diamantes. I looked like Lady Gaga in the 'Bad Romance' video. Nice to know I did it all those years before Gaga.

I had to shave every single tiny bit of hair off my body

when I was dressing up. You wouldn't be able to find a single hair. The last thing you'd want is to be a hairy woman.

STEPHEN

I was back working for Toni and Guy in Wimbledon but I was getting itchy feet again. Then one day I saw an advert for a hairdressing job in Dubai and I thought, 'I'm going to go for that'. Then I turned to my friends Carly and Lucy and said, 'Where's Dubai?'

During my interview this woman said to me, 'Now, you know Dubai is a Muslim country and it's illegal to be gay there, don't you?' I replied, 'Being gay doesn't define who I am. I don't care if there aren't any gay bars, I'm going there to work.' And with that I signed a two-year contract.

I was imagining myself living on this beautiful desert island and spending days lying in the sun drinking cocktails. I was so excited.

At Heathrow airport I met a girl called Lorna who was heading out to do the same thing. After checking in we headed straight to a bar. We were chattering away about how amazing it was going to be. *It wasn't.*

When we landed in Dubai it was *awful*. This paradise I'd imagined was anything but. We were met by a girl, Jane, from the company who immediately took our passports away from us, which is never a good sign.

Jane took us to the apartment where we were going to be living and when we got there it was a fucking state. It was filthy and there were cockroaches running around. Lorna was as horrified as me and I turned round and said to Jane, 'We're not staying here. It's a shithole.'

She calmed us down and said we only had to stay there until we got our own place, so we agreed to suck it up for a couple of days. As she walked out Jane said, 'See you at work tomorrow at 9am.' The company weren't even going to give us a day or two to wander around and find our feet.

After that things went from bad to worse *very* quickly. People were quite unfriendly towards us and we were expected to work really long hours. So much for an extended holiday.

Then, one night, about five months after we'd arrived, Lorna and I were out in a bar and this bloke wouldn't leave her alone. He was really hassling her so I told him where to go and he threw his drink over me. I threw a drink back over him and with that he hit a bottle over my head.

The bottle didn't break so he smashed it on the bar and then tried to attack Lorna with it. Thankfully she put her arms up to protect her face just in time but he still ended up slashing her arms.

The police were called and when they arrived they arrested Lorna because they said she was dressed like a prostitute. She was wearing jeans and a T-shirt! Then they arrested me because I'd said 'fuck' and cursing is illegal over there.

We were taken to the police station with blood pouring out of our wounds and forced to sign these papers that were written in Arabic which said, amongst other things, that we wouldn't sue the man who'd attacked us.

Once they were satisfied we weren't going to take any further action they finally let us go to the hospital. Because we'd been drinking the doctors and nurses were really dismissive and unhelpful. They managed to stop my head bleeding but they did a crap job of patching it up and I've still got a big scar now. They also stitched up poor Lorna's arm without giving her any anaesthetic whatsoever. Can you imagine how painful that must have been?

The following day Lorna and I tried to hand our notices in to the salon and we were told we had to give three months' notice and pay £1,500 to get out of our contracts early. There was no way we could put up with another three months of that shit.

We came up with a plan where Lorna would go to her doctor and say she was really depressed and worried that the man who attacked her was coming after her.

Her doctor referred to be a specialist in a nearby hospital. We were due to pass the British Embassy on the way to her appointment so we decided to pop in and see if they could do anything to help us. We spoke to a really nice lady who told us that by law the company we were working for were allowed to withhold our passports from us, which wasn't what we wanted to hear.

She asked what our plan was and when we told her we were on the way to the hospital she looked at the name on the letter and said, 'You don't want to go there. That's a secure unit.' We both burst into tears because we realized we were in serious trouble.

Lorna and I were left with no choice but to work out our notice period and make the best of things. Three months later we were standing at the airport ready to get our flight home and Jane turned up on a moped and finally handed us back our passports. We'd managed to last for eight months in total, but it was eight months of hell.

I was so broke I flew back with Bangladeshi Airlines and was delayed for eight hours. I was honestly wondering if I'd ever get out of the bloody country.

I was also in agony because I'd jumped off a table doing a Michael Jackson impression at our leaving party the night before, and I'd been too scared to go to hospital in case they said I wasn't allowed to fly. I later found out I had a broken ankle.

Lorna and I were so pissed off that when we landed back in London we took the company credit card, went down Bond Street and spent £3,000. I had this really swollen foot but I was squeezing it into these Prada shoes going, 'I love them! I'll have them!'

When we got back, me and Lorna phoned Toni and Guy's head office to see if we could get our jobs back. They said they could offer us a job in either Australia or Brighton. The last thing I wanted to do at that time was leave the country again, so Brighton it was.

Lorna and I both moved down together and we're still really close now. Her daughter Sia Willow is my goddaughter, and she's amazing.

I arrived at Toni and Guy in 2001 with my leg bandaged up. I remember sitting downstairs in the salon waiting for the manager to show me around and this bloke came strutting down the stairs and swished passed me. I thought, 'Bloody hell, do you want some onions with that mince?' I also thought, 'Look at that lovely bum'.

And that, ladies and gentlemen, is the first time I ever met Chris.

CHRIS

Stephen and I did chat a bit but we hung around in different crowds and I left Toni and Guy not long after he joined. So we didn't really properly get to know each other until much later on.

STEPHEN

I stayed in Brighton for the next two and a half years and I had a great time. But I started to really miss London so I moved back up to Vauxhall with my mate Lee. He went to the same school as me but he was a few years below me. I used to see him around Sittingbourne and I always wondered if he was gay.

I had some of the best years of my life hanging out with him and we made a pact that we'd never tell anyone else about the naughty stuff we got up to. And we've kept that promise to this day.

I'd just started seeing a guy who I really thought was the one, but I don't think I was in the right place to have a proper relationship at that time. We were together for two years and I was heartbroken when we split up because he was such a nice guy, but it wasn't to be. I always wondered if he was the one who got away.

CHRIS

As well as me, obviously.

STEPHEN

Obviously. After we split up I went back to India to do some more travelling. When I arrived back in London and went back to work life felt like it didn't mean anything. I was thinking, 'All I do it cut hair and pander to rich women in Kensington.'

I hit 40 and I thought, 'I'm going to go back to Brighton'. I wanted my life to become smaller and more manageable. I didn't want to be moving from flat to flat. I wanted to aim towards getting my own place. And I wanted a dog.

I got my job back at Toni and Guy in Brighton and my mum moved down at the same time. We got a place together but it was only small so I was sleeping on the sofa. I knew it was only temporary and I had a plan in my head of where I wanted to be, but that meant saving up some money.

The great thing about being in London is that you can get away with anything because you're pretty anonymous. Unless you got off with everyone you work with like I did, of course. But when I moved to Brighton I cottoned on fast to the fact that everyone knew each other, and if you got off with someone everyone would know about it. That made me more aware of what I was doing, and with who.

CHRIS

You could definitely get away with being naughtier in London because you meet different people every day. I don't go out that much anymore but when I do I can guarantee the same people will be in the same bars that were in there five years ago. And people will still gossip about you.

STEPHEN

When Grindr first came out it was incredible because it made things so much easier. But probably not really the kind of place you meet someone who wants a long-term relationship.

Before Grindr I loved internet dating. I never got nervous on dates. I used to really enjoy them.

CHRIS

You had to be careful about which dating sites you used though. The gay dating scene can be so confusing. There are lists for everything. You've got bears, cubs, twinks, muscle

Marys and leather queens. Then you've got tops, bottoms and versatiles. You've also got power bottoms and lazy tops.

There's also the handkerchief code. This dates back to the 1970s leather queens. They'd have a hanky in their back pocket and one side meant you were a top, and the other side meant you were a bottom. There were also different colours depending on what they were into.

You've also got different degrees of gay. You've got gold, silver and bronze. It's like the Olympics of gayness. Bronze means you've done everything with a woman but you've now fully come out of the closet. Then you've got silver, which means you've only kissed a woman and you're gay. Then you've got gold, which means the only contact you've had with a woman's bits is when you were born. They're basically different degrees of how close you've been to a woman's bits.

Then, just to add another layer, you've got a platinum gay. That's a gay men who's never had any action with a woman and was delivered by C-section. Honest to God.

I'm bronze because I've done everything with a woman and I was born naturally.

STEPHEN

Me too. It's a minefield. I started off online dating on Match.com and that gave me the confidence to get on Grindr, which seemed quite intimidating at first. And everyone knows what it's there for and it's all very honest.

CHRIS

It's difficult because you always put up your best pictures of yourself on sites or apps and there's always a chance someone will be disappointed when you turn up to meet them. But it's just so much easier to date like that. With the lifestyles we have these days people don't have the time to go and hang out in bars and hope we meet someone.

STEPHEN

These days you go to a bar to have a laugh with your mates and you're not really on the pull. You can just go on Tinder or Grindr for that.

I went out on a date to Wagamama with this guy I met on Grindr once, and he also happened to know Chris. We both ordered our food and he went for firecracker chicken, which I'd never heard of before. When the food arrived he was in the loo so I decided to try a bit of his. It was so nice I kept on eating it, and before I knew it his plate looked a bit sparse. I did that thing where you spread the food around to make it look like there's more than there is, but it still looked really meagre. He came back and sat down and started eating what was left of his meal and neither of us said anything. I thought I'd better pay for the meal because he'd barely eaten anything, so he must have thought I was really generous.

CHRIS

I saw that guy the following week and I said to him, 'Have you been on a date with a guy called Stephen? And did you notice that half of your food was missing?'

STEPHEN

I generally eat the same whenever I eat out because I get scared of getting something I won't enjoy. What a waste of money if you don't like it. I tend to eat the same things over and over again because then you know what you're getting.

CHRIS

Growing up, the only way you could get in contact with other gay people was via the classified ads in the local paper. The heading would say 'Him for Him' and you had to write a letter to the guy you liked and send it to a postbox. Then you'd wait for him to reply to you and it went on for *days*.

I met up with this guy when I was in my late teens after we met through the classifieds.

I was sitting in a café in the Octagon Centre in High Wycombe and this man walked in who looked like a total pervert. He had slicked-back hair and he was wearing a shell suit. He came over to me and said, 'Are you Chris?' My brain was screaming, 'Say no! Say no!' And then this timid little 'yes' came out of my mouth. I couldn't get rid of him. I knew his whole bloody life story within an hour.

I'd got the bus over to meet him so when he offered me a lift home, I accepted. I realize I probably gave him the wrong idea but it *was* raining. He wanted to come inside and meet my mum so I made an excuse about her being unwell. I never saw him again, thankfully.

STEPHEN
Jesus, I bet you didn't rush back to the classifieds after that?

CHRIS
No.

STEPHEN
Thank God for online dating and apps. We'd never have got together otherwise. I'd been single for a while and one day I was looking on Grindr and I spotted a picture of Chris. He was lying on the sofa with a cap on and he looked really cute.

I texted my friend Lorna and said, 'Do you remember Chris from Brighton? Is he a yes or no?' And she said, 'Chris as in Christina? No!' I sent her the picture of him and said, 'Look at him now!' And she was like, 'Bloody hell, go for it!'

I contacted Chris and we started chatting over Grindr for a few days.

CHRIS

I was all confused because he said his name was Stephen, but everyone at Toni and Guy called him George because there were two Stephens.

STEPHEN

We arranged to meet up outside the All Saints shop in Brighton and the first thing we did was go to the sunbed shop to top up our tans. While we were waiting for the beds to be free, Chris said to me, 'You're quite cute actually,' and tried to put his hand up my shorts. He wasn't a shy one.

We arranged to meet at Brighton station for our first 'proper' date. I'd been to London a couple of days before and bought this lovely Prada shirt specially.

CHRIS

Can I just say, Stephen can no longer fit into that shirt but he's kept it because he reckons he'll get back into it one day. *Of course* he will.

STEPHEN

The buttonholes are on my nipples now. I'm gutted because it's such a nice shirt but it looks like I've borrowed it from a twelve-year-old.

I thought he would guess we were probably going up to London for the day so he'd dress up a bit, but when he turned up he was wearing jeans and a vest.

CHRIS

I was actually wearing some pale mustard rolled-up chinos and a white vest. It was summer and I thought we were going to be going for a few drinks in Soho or something. I didn't know he was going to take me somewhere posh. I wasn't sure if he even liked me at that point, so I wasn't expecting him to splash out loads of money.

STEPHEN

You must have known I liked you when I leant over and kissed you on the train journey up to London?

CHRIS

That was on the journey back.

STEPHEN

So it was. We got the train to London Bridge and walked down to the river. It was dead romantic. Then we went to the Oxo Tower for drinks. Chris ordered a mocktail. When he went to the loo I called the waitress over and told her to put a vodka in it.

CHRIS

The drink was lovely and when I finished it I said I'd like the same sort of thing again but with vodka in it. Obviously Stephen was thinking, 'Fuck, it's going to taste exactly the same'.

We got a bit drunk and we went dancing at a club called Escape on Old Compton Street in Soho afterwards. We got the last train back to Brighton and we had such a laugh. Even though he really got on my nerves at times, Stephen could always make me laugh.

STEPHEN

Until the laughter turned to tears. We did have a few good months together though. We used to go on little dates to the beach.

CHRIS

Stephen used to come and meet me after work and we'd go out for picnics or walks. We were in that lovely early relationship bubble and I think we both thought it was going to go somewhere.

But it all started going a bit tits up during our first holiday. Stephen can't read maps and we had a big argument on the way to Gatwick because he was panicking about which lane he had to be in. I could see the holiday ending in tears before it had even started.

To be fair, we were lucky to get to Egypt at all. Our plane travelled for two and a half hours and then the pilot announced there was something wrong with it and we had to turn around and go all the way back. We were delayed by five hours and all they gave us was some water and a biscuit.

STEPHEN

Chris started telling people the phalange on the plane had broken, like he was Phoebe from *Friends*.

CHRIS

We got there just in time for New Year, and we met a couple called Sammy and Gat on the coach transfer to the hotel. We ended up hanging out with them all the time and it was brilliant.

STEPHEN

We got totally tricked while we were there. This big hunky bloke was walking around the pool, and he said to us, 'Would you like a massage?' Chris and I were like, 'Fuck, yeeeeahhhh!' We booked up straight away, but when we turned up to the spa we were greeted by two *women*. He was clearly total massage bait.

Oh God, do you remember when we went on that donut that was being pulled along by a speedboat? They took us out so far out we couldn't see land anymore and I said to Chris, 'They're going to murder us.'

The guys driving the boat started going really fast and I went flying off the rubber ring. I was in the air for long enough to think, 'When I hit that water I'm going to break my neck'. Then I went crashing down and my shorts came clean off. I came back to the surface and shouted, 'I'm naked! I'm fucking *naked*!'

CHRIS

He was there one minute and gone the next and then he was screaming his head off.

STEPHEN

We also went on a banana boat. We'd met this 70-year-old man called Gordon and we convinced him to come out with us, telling him what a laugh it would be. The minute the banana hit a certain speed Gordon fell off the back into the water. We spent about half an hour trying to drag him back onto the bloody boat and he looked at me and said, 'I think this has been a really bad idea.'

CHRIS

Gordon and Glenda were lovely but Glenda was really good at turning a cheery conversation into some quite dark. We'd be having dinner and Gordon would be telling us the story of how they met and Glenda would say, 'That reminds me of the time that shark killed that baby.'

We'd be having a lovely time and she'd say something really awful and depressing to totally bring the mood down. She was the voice of doom.

STEPHEN

That was a great holiday. Even though we didn't speak for the last three nights. We fell out because we were having a play fight in our room and I said to him, 'Chris, stop this because one of us is going to get hurt and it isn't going to be me.' He kept coming at me like a snappy little Jack Russell so I pushed him away and he scratched his knee on the wall.

CHRIS

It bloody hurt!

STEPHEN

Gordon used to write poems and one night he wrote one for me about something stupid I'd said over dinner, and that caused another argument.

CHRIS

Only because it was when we weren't speaking and you're such a bitchy little queen that you wouldn't let me read it. You showed it to everyone else to wind me up and you wouldn't let me see it. And you kept doing that gross thing where you piss yourself.

STEPHEN

I do piss myself a lot on holiday. Usually on the sun lounger on the beach. I get up every fourth or fifth wee to rinse myself off in the sea and then I lie back down and have another beer.

CHRIS

I'm a fun holiday partner. I'll be on the beach doing cartwheels or playing 'guess the dance moves'. It's my favourite holiday game. It basically involves me doing the dance routine to a well-known song and other holidaymakers have to guess which one it is.

STEPHEN

You did a good impression of Lady Godiva on that holiday. Not Lady Godiva. Who do I mean? Lady La-Da?

CHRIS

Lady Gaga?

STEPHEN

Yeah, that's the one.

CHRIS

We didn't go on family holidays when we were kids. The only one I went on was to Great Yarmouth and it was fantastic. We were in this really skanky static caravan for a week but the campsite had a climbing frame and a clubhouse and it was right near the beach.

The first time I went abroad was when I went to Gran Canaria for a week with my boyfriend Paul. It was a disaster. I put on loads of sun cream but I still burnt really badly on the first day and I ended up with a white handprint on my chest where the sun cream had stuck to me. I looked like a pillock. I couldn't go out in the sun the following day so I decided to go and get drunk and I ended up with alcohol poisoning. Then a couple of days later I got food poisoning.

We hired a car and it broke down. I didn't drive back then so Paul had to try and get it started while I pushed it. I was really pleased because all my nails had grown in the sun, but when Paul finally managed to get the car started and drove off my hands slid off the boot and every single one of my nails broke. And I fell on my face.

STEPHEN

That does sound like a disaster. We didn't go on holiday when I was a kid either. We had a couple of breaks in the UK but we didn't go abroad.

We went to the New Forest when I was about four and me, Paul, Denise and mum were all lying in this tent when a horse poked its head through the opening and my mum screamed her head off.

She got us all ready in our nice clothes one night and then she couldn't find me. Apparently I was in a field covered in cow shit. She lost me again the following night and she found me in the kids' swimming pool, soaking wet.

My uncle Bill took us all to Ramsgate once, and the first time I went abroad was when I went to visit my dad in Holland. My first proper holiday was to Bodrum in Turkey with Denise when I was 20. I remember being really nervous about flying for the first time but I loved it.

CHRIS

We started bickering more and more after our holiday in Egypt but I was still hopeful it could work out. Then we spent Valentine's Day together and it was a massive letdown.

STEPHEN

You bought me a rose, didn't you?

CHRIS

Yes. And a card.

STEPHEN

I remember walking down the street to meet you and seeing you holding the rose and I didn't have anything. But we had said we weren't going to get each other anything?

CHRIS

Just because we *said* we weren't going to that didn't mean we actually *weren't*. The idea is to surprise each other, but I guess it wasn't much of a surprise when you turned up empty handed.

STEPHEN

You were so fucked off and you said, 'What? You didn't get me *nuffink*? Well you had better go and get something for me *now*.' You screeched up outside the local Tesco Metro and sent me in to buy you a present. Because it was Valentine's Day there were no roses or chocolates left so I got an Easter egg and some cat food. I thought, 'Well, he'll like the Easter egg because he likes chocolate. And he'll like the cat food because it's saved him a bit of money.'

CHRIS

He'd already bought dinner for us to eat at mine earlier in the day.

STEPHEN

See? I did get you something.

CHRIS

Yeah, you got one of those Dine in for Two meals from M&S for a tenner. You got mussels for the starter, which I don't like. I can't remember what the main was but I didn't like that either. And you got your favourite dessert. So basically you bought a Valentine's dinner for yourself that I could barely eat and I got cat food and an Easter egg.

STEPHEN

That wasn't a great night. I think we both knew things were going a bit downhill. One minute it was all going swimmingly, and the next minute it wasn't. We were together for about eight months in total but the last three months weren't great.

CHRIS

I'd already been approached by *Gogglebox* at this point and we'd both agreed to go ahead with it.

STEPHEN

I'll be honest – when Chris first explained the format to me and asked if I wanted to do it I said, 'That sounds shit!'

CHRIS

On paper it does sound quite basic.

STEPHEN

I never, ever, for one minute imagined how good it was going to be. Even when we were filming it I had no idea whether it would be popular or not. The first series was only four episodes long and we were just messing about. The show started off on Channel 4 on Wednesday nights at 10pm. We were one of the originals on the show, along with June and Leon, Sandy and Sandra, the Siddiquis, Steph and Dom, the Tappers and the Michaels.

CHRIS

To start with we did think how weird it was that there was a camera in my living room, but we genuinely forgot it was there after a little while. We were totally being ourselves, but we were also really nervous about how we'd be portrayed.

STEPHEN

I was concerned that we could come across badly. You could easily say something that could be taken out of context.

CHRIS

When you're in your own home your mouth does run away with you so every time we thought we'd gone too far we said the 'c' word so we knew they wouldn't be able to use that clip.

STEPHEN

It's a reality show of sorts, so they could easily have stitched us up and made us look really stupid. Not that Chris needs a massive amount of help, mind.

CHRIS

That's rich coming from you. You like to give people the impression you're the clever one but I'm the one who got an A in my Creative Arts GCSE.

STEPHEN

Right up until the first episode went out on air that March I was worried about how the show would come across. Then when I saw it I thought, 'This is really, really funny'.

When the first episode aired it started trending on Twitter straight away. It showed us watching a programme about meteorites that had fallen to Earth. Chris popped out to the kitchen and when he came back in I said to him, 'You want to see what this women is doing. She's going out in the snow looking for meteorites. This crank is minge deep in snow.'

That line went crazy on Twitter. People were making memes of it. Someone made an Ecard where these two women were on the phone to each other and one is saying to the other, 'Hey, do you fancy coming out and getting minge deep in snow?'

CHRIS

It's funny how things catch on. We were watching this guy on some drama making a bomb and I said to Stephen, 'Everyone loves a bad boy,' and he replied, 'Yeah, but not a fucking terrorist though Chris.' Then it went quiet and Stephen turned to me and said, 'Would you date Hitler?'

STEPHEN

One of the funniest times was when you were eating that brioche bun and you started munching on your tooth. But it didn't get shown.

Brioches are really soft but I could hear Chris crunching something and I jokingly said, 'Are you eating your teeth or something?' and he went, 'Oh my God, I am!'

CHRIS

It was when I was having my veneers redone so I had some temporary ones attached. As soon as Stephen mentioned how noisy I was being it registered that chocolate chips shouldn't be that crunchy.

This was around the time there was a lot of rubbish in the papers about the show being edited and us being told what to say, which was absolute crap. That was really annoying. As soon as the series started people started claiming we'd been scripted.

STEPHEN

People are still convinced the show is scripted. But how could you script it? We just watch TV and talk rubbish.

Chapter Seven

BOX CLEVER

Chris: 'I don't think much about "me" as a person has changed.'
Stephen: 'Apart from the fact you're now dripping in Louis Vuitton.'

CHRIS

I remember the day the first ever episode of *Gogglebox* was due to air. We were in London for the day and I was sat looking out the window on the train back and it suddenly hit me that all those people in all those houses could be watching us later. It was quite scary.

I can't remember the first time we got recognized after the show came out but it would probably have been somewhere in Brighton.

STEPHEN

I remember walking around London with Chris just after the series started and this woman stopped us and said, 'Are you two on *Gogglebox*? I love that show!' And I thought it was so odd. I like being recognized though, because lots of good-looking straight men talk to us.

CHRIS

They'll say, 'My girlfriend loves you. Can I have my photo taken with you?'

STEPHEN

The straight lads get really flirty sometimes. Especially in Scotland, for some reason. They also do the best chips and gravy in Glasgow.

It's nice because younger people come up to us now. I remember someone saying to me once that the older you get the more invisible you get, and it's true, especially on the gay scene. So I think being on TV has made us a bit more visible and it's given us a little boost. Before, I was invisible to teenagers and twentysomethings, but now they all ask for selfies.

CHRIS

We get recognized much more when we're together, and we seem to get recognized more up north.

BOX CLEVER

STEPHEN

The northerners are great. They've got no qualms about marching straight up to you and asking for a photo. I think people down south play it a bit cooler.

CHRIS

I was on holiday in Fuerteventura and this guy told me it had gone round the whole resort that I was there and everyone wanted their photo taken with me. That was surreal.

The weirdest thing is when people look at you and talk about you but don't approach you. Quite often, I'll be in a bar and someone will start chatting to me but they won't let on they know I'm on *Gogglebox*. Then about ten minutes into a conversation they'll say, 'By the way, I love the show.' I also find it weird when people recognize you but they don't approach you. They just stare!

STEPHEN

I get that though. Sometimes when you see someone famous you think you know them but you can't place them.

I remember seeing this guy on *The X Factor* and I thought, 'I know you. I think I've shagged you.' Then I realized it was Olly Murs and I'd seen him on *Deal or No Deal* a couple of years before.

I think people do the same thing with us. They think we're familiar but they might not click where they know us from.

Sometimes people will say hello to me and then look really confused as if they're trying to work out who I am.

We do get asked for photos in some odd places. We were at a motorway service station a while ago and we were shovelling McDonald's down. . .

CHRIS

And Stephen's not the prettiest at eating.

STEPHEN

This woman came over and shoved her really tiny kids next to us and took a photo while we had burger hanging out of our mouths. That would *not* have been a nice photo.

CHRIS

We've been really lucky that pretty much everyone has been positive towards us. Although we did have a Twitter troll once that told us we looked like Belisha beacons.

STEPHEN

She fucked off quite quickly though. I scrolled down her home page and there was a photo of her getting chucked out of Iceland. I think that says it all.

CHRIS

The thing with Stephen is that he'll respond when someone says something nasty.

BOX CLEVER

STEPHEN

Not anymore. The big lesson I've learnt from Twitter is to ignore the criticism. The moment you reply you've engaged with that person and that's what they want. Now I just block arseholes.

The only time someone's said something nasty to my face is when I was walking through my village. A car pulled up next to me and this bloke wound down the window and said, 'Oi, mate, are you on that show, *Gogglebox*? You're a c**t!' I started really laughing and said, 'I know!' so he started laughing and drove off. I thought it was hilarious.

Sometimes I am surprised we get such a good response. I mean, Stephen's not the most subtle of people, is he? When they showed the John Lewis advert with the little penguin who gets a girlfriend Stephen said, 'He's going to get stuck in that tonight.' I mean, that *could* offend people.

STEPHEN

I think our banter is just what other people would say, and that's why a lot of the straight boys like us. We were watching a programme earlier this year where this couple were getting down to it and Chris shouted, 'Ruin her!' at the TV. That's the sort of thing you'd expect a group of straight lads to shout, not a gay guy.

CHRIS

I did get a bit of flack when we were watching *Aliens* with Sigourney Weaver. She was shooting her gun really aggressively and I said, 'Lesbian'. The amount of tweets I got after that was ridiculous. A lot of people were really angry with me about it. But she did look like a lesbian. What's wrong with that?

STEPHEN

What about when you retweeted a paedo?

CHRIS

Oh God. We get so many people asking us to retweet things and someone tweeted me saying, 'Please can you retweet this? This person has done more for children than most charities.'

I retweeted it and two seconds later someone messaged me to say I needed to take it down because the man in question was a massive perv. I was a lot more careful after that. I always read tweets first now.

A lot of criminals all look the same, don't they? You rarely get a good-looking mugshot, do you? They're always really scary. But when you see old photos of people like Myra Hindley smiling you think, 'Well, you'd never have known.'

There was that bloke in America that got a modelling contract off the back of his arrest picture. He was named as the world's hottest convict. He didn't kill anyone or do anything really bad. But I think he got done for having a gun, which isn't great.

STEPHEN

It's not ideal.

CHRIS

I can't really be bothered with Twitter. Stephen's got RSI from using Facebook and Twitter. Although, if *Gogglebox* is on I do go on Twitter so see what people are saying about it. I can't be arsed with Instagram either. Everyone keeps saying I should set up an account for Buddy and Rusty, but I can't be arsed to do my own, let alone theirs.

I'm even thinking about coming off Facebook because I'm so annoyed about everyone commenting on politics and stuff when they don't really know what they're talking about. The worst thing is when people put something like, 'Feeling annoyed' and everyone replies, 'What's up hun?' It's attention seeking.

STEPHEN

I'm tempted to take Facebook off my phone and just check it once a day when I get home from work. I'm constantly looking at what everyone is up to and it takes up so much time. The thing is, I've got friends in Australia and America and around Europe and that's how I keep in touch with them.

I find it weird when people post things about their dead relatives. Surely that stuff should be private? I don't like people wishing me happy birthday on there either. It's only because they can't be bothered to send me a card.

CHRIS

And I don't need to know what people are having for dinner.

STEPHEN

I do post photos of my food sometimes, I must admit. But only when I'm out somewhere nice. I also post a lot of photos of drinks. There does have to be a line. I once wrote a post on Twitter telling everyone I was on a train. I had to have a word with myself after that.

CHRIS

I think it's okay to post food pictures if you're going to a nice restaurant, but I don't want to see a photo of someone's beans on toast or cottage pie. The problem is, everyone is a nosy bastard so they do look at that shit.

STEPHEN

But it's only self. . .

CHRIS

Importance?

BOX CLEVER

STEPHEN

No, like self-promotion in a way? Like the way everyone's blogging now.

CHRIS

Everyone is an Instagram star or a blogger these days, aren't they? That all drives me mad.

STEPHEN

Some of them are really annoying but my friend Lorna Luxe has got a good blog. She used to be a trolley dolly and she started photographing herself in nice outfits against white backgrounds, and that became her key look. She writes very well and she's become really successful. She does put the work in though.

CHRIS

It is crazy though. When we were growing up you had to have a talent to be famous, whereas anyone can be famous now.

STEPHEN

Andy Warhol said everyone will have their 15 minutes of fame and he was right.

CHRIS

That 'Charlie bit my finger' video has been watched more times than Princess Diana's funeral.

STEPHEN

Someone told me that if you get over a million hits on YouTube you automatically get £20,000.

CHRIS

I thought our 'everyone loves a bad boy' conversation had been viewed well over a million times. Where's our cash?

I get sick of game requests on Facebook. Why would I want to build a farm in Farmville? I have trouble coping with my real garden, let alone having a pretend one with animals and stuff. How does anyone have time?

STEPHEN

I can't get the whole Pokemon Go thing at all. I haven't even looked at it.

CHRIS

I can't believe people are falling off cliffs and getting run over trying to catch some stupid thing that isn't real. I think it's sad. It's the same with Candy Crush, although I did get into it for a while when I was working in a salon and I had time to fill. Now I'm far too busy and important.

I think because we were so busy filming *Gogglebox* and it was all so new Stephen and I stopped going out on dates together. We kind of forgot about the romantic side of things. Stephen was also taking the mickey out of me all the time on the show and I felt like he was putting me down quite

216

a lot. There was a certain amount of pressure to be funny and I became the stooge.

STEPHEN

It was only banter, but it didn't sit well with two people who were going out with each other. It would have been fine if we were friends but I probably overstepped the mark at times. He was just as good at giving it back at times though, and I didn't get upset.

CHRIS

You've got thicker skin.

STEPHEN

To be fair, you did announce in one of the first episodes that I had a small dick. We were watching *Embarrassing Bodies* and I said, 'I wish I'd gone on there to get my foreskin removed,' and you replied, 'But then everyone would know you've got a small willy.' I did see the funny side though. If banter is funny I'll laugh, but if it's nasty and bitchy, forget it.

I can handle most piss-taking but Chris used to get really offended. He's got a lot better as time's gone on though.

CHRIS

It was difficult at the time because we were supposed to be spending nice time together as a couple and he was ripping the piss out of me constantly. And we were annoying each other about stupid things. Stephen can be very lazy and that got to me. He's also very generous in lots of ways but selfish in others. He's very generous with his farts, for instance. I often felt like I had to make all the effort. He was still living with him mum when we were dating and he didn't drive so I was always going to pick him up so he could hang out at my place. I reckon he was just trying to escape his mum.

STEPHEN

No, that's not true. I love being around my mum. But I suppose I didn't have many friends in Brighton at that time. I knew some people from Toni and Guy but you were like my best mate really. And the longer we kept seeing each other I started to really like you. Even if your manic-ness drove me a bit mad at times.

I loved the fact you were so 'out there' and you didn't care what people thought about you. Believe it or not, when I met you I was still having issues with being gay. I never denied that I was gay to anyone but I didn't offer up the information and still didn't feel totally comfortable with it.

Being with you taught me how to be myself. You were having a laugh and not giving a shit and you were so happy in your own skin. I completely and utterly admired you for it. Unbeknown to him, he helped me to be more accepting of who I was.

CHRIS

Stephen is very blunt and that was hard at times. I can be blunt but I know when to switch it on and off, whereas Stephen doesn't. If I ever needed advice now I would never go to Stephen for it.

STEPHEN

My answer to everything is, 'Tell 'em to fuck off!'

CHRIS

And that's not always what you want to hear.

STEPHEN

I think I'm good at solving other people's problems but not my own.

CHRIS

That's because you're not emotionally attached to the situation. It's like when I'm giving advice to my clients. If someone says their husband is being an arsehole I'm like, 'Just leave him.' But when you're in that situation it's much harder to make decisions.

It sounds like we drove each other crazy but it wasn't like that all the time. We did have some really good times.

STEPHEN

We did. We had a lot of fun. But the longer we were together the more we realized that we weren't compatible, didn't we? We both agreed that we weren't going to work as a couple. I'm not big fan of going out and you still enjoyed it back then. I felt like we were too different.

I was dreading having the break-up conversation but I took Chris out for a Thai meal and said, 'It's not really working, it is?' and he replied, 'NO'.

We had a good chat and we agreed that if we're both single in 20 years' time we'll share a house and potter around garden centres together.

CHRIS

We'll have separate rooms, obviously, because we're not going to do anything with each other. We'll go and look at plants during the day and eat dinner together in front of the TV.

STEPHEN

Well that's something to look forward to, isn't it? We split up just after the end of the first series and we tweeted about it as if we were some famous Hollywood couple. You know, 'Just to let all our fans know. . .' I only had about 7,000 followers then. I don't think anyone picked up on the tweet anyway, and all these years later people still think we're together.

BOX CLEVER

CHRIS

The funniest thing is when people tweet and say, 'I want a relationship like Chris and Stephen from *Gogglebox*.' You bloody don't.

After we broke up I really didn't want to see Stephen. We'd spent so much time arguing I felt like I needed a break, so I ignored him for a while.

STEPHEN

When we had that chat in the Thai restaurant we agreed we'd stay mates whatever happened. But Chris's version of 'staying friends' was defriending me on Facebook. So I blocked him.

I didn't hear from him at all so it was clear he'd decided to cut me out, but I wasn't having any of it. We weren't compatible as boyfriends but I wasn't going to let him *not* be friends with me. So I forced my way back into his affections.

CHRIS

And now I can't get rid of him. The main reason I defriended Stephen was because he started seeing Daniel. He kept putting up pictures of them together and I thought, 'Enough is enough.' I'd log on to Facebook and my feed would say 'Stephen's added photos' and it would be him and Daniel look all cosy and happy. So I ditched him. But then he wouldn't fucking leave me alone.

He turned up at my house one day out of the blue and when I said he couldn't come in he said, 'Oh fuck off, make me a cup of tea,' and walked right in.

After that he start popping round regularly and in the end I said to him, 'You can't keep coming round here,' and he said, 'Don't be so fucking stupid.' I'm sure it's only because he didn't have any other friends.

STEPHEN

I *kind of* met Daniel online. We were both at Hove Town Hall in the queue for parking permits one day and we didn't speak but I thought he was lovely. When I got home and logged onto Plenty of Fish he popped up. I messaged him saying, 'Did I see you in Hove Town Hall today?' and he suggested we meet up for a drink sometime.

A week later I had to go back to Hove Town Hall to sort out some other parking stuff and he was there again. I think we were supposed to meet there. It was destiny.

CHRIS

It was. It's so weird how things like that happen.

STEPHEN

Daniel and I arranged to go out that night and I picked him up in my yellow Mini. He didn't do his seat belt up and I said, 'I'd rethink that if I was you. I only passed my test four weeks ago.' I suggested we went to this nice pub out in the sticks and weirdly he was going to suggest the same place. See, it was fate. We had dinner and I was all giddy because I fancied him so much, but I also thought he was a bit of a snot. He was sitting really upright and eating his dinner all nicely and I was wolfing mine down like I hadn't eaten for three days. I had no idea if was interested and I felt like it was pretty touch and go. I wasn't sure if he'd see past the end of his nose and see how great I am, but thankfully he did and we had a kiss at the end of the night. I know it sounds odd but I wouldn't usually snog on a first date. I think a peck on the cheek is enough.

One of my most romantic nights out with Daniel was when I took him to the Oxo Tower. That's where I take all my dates. But poor Chris only got a drink and Daniel got a three-course meal. I told Daniel the whole night was all a ploy to make him fall in love with me and I think it worked because we were pretty much inseparable after that.

CHRIS

I met Tony through Gaydar and we chatted on there for ages before we got together. Probably around a year or so.

Then he moved to my area of Brighton so he popped up on Grindr. We started chatting and he happened to be going to a comedy night called Bent Double at a place called Komedia on the same night as me.

I kept an eye out for him but when I saw him he was

hanging out with all these big burly blokes – who I later found out were from the Brighton Gay Men's Chorus, which Tony is a part of – I thought, 'He wouldn't be interested in me. I can't be bothered.' He didn't see me that evening but he messaged me the next day asking what had happened to me.

It was only when I was at a charity event for World AIDS Day in a pub a few months later that we properly met and talked. But I'd already copped off with some other bloke that night so it wasn't ideal.

I ended up seeing him three times that week but the next time we bumped into each other I was on a date with the other guy I'd been snogging and I thought to myself, 'I think I'm ruining my chances here'.

I then saw him again a couple nights later and thankfully that time I was just out with some friends and I wasn't snogging anyone! We had a quick chat and I said, 'We really do need to meet up.'

Tony says that's when something in his heart began to click, but I was trying to play hard to get so I was going off and chatting to other people. I knew I really liked him though, and we kept drifting back together.

We arranged to have some drinks, and nearly three years later we're still going strong. It just felt right. Things fell into place and it was effortless. Tony is such an amazing person.

I think Tony came along at the right time because I went through a phase of being a bit of a slut for a while and I was so bored of it. I was in a bar called Legends in Brighton when I was about 27 and I was so proud of the fact there was no one in there I'd slept with. By the end of the night I spotted three guys I'd copped off with before. They were all friends with each other so they were all stood in a group chatting. I thought to myself, 'Oh. My. God. I don't want to be *that* person.' Then a few minutes later I thought, 'Yeah, I do', and I snogged someone else. I didn't calm down for quite some time after that.

STEPHEN

You definitely make more of an effort to impress someone early on. When Daniel went to Pride the first year we started dating, I knew he'd be feeling ropey the following morning so I took him round a Nero's coffee and some croissants. I wouldn't bloody do that now.

CHRIS

I never know when it's the right time to put a kiss on a text when you start seeing someone.

STEPHEN

I'll put a put a kiss on a text pretty much straight away. But I don't rush things. I don't think you should say I love you until you really feel it. If someone said it to me and I didn't feel the same way I wouldn't say it back. It's got to be the right time.

CHRIS

Tony used to tell me he loved me 100 times a day and in the end I said to him, 'You need to stop. It's too much.'

Tony and I are really different in some ways because I'm not a very emotional person and he is. He cries at everything and he says I haven't had an emotion since 1983. That's why I think it makes me feel a bit uncomfortable telling him I love him.

In some ways, you miss out on things when you're with someone for years because the excitement goes. But then you're left with something lovely and you develop a really deep bond. I do love that time when you can't get enough of each other though. You know when you pine for the other person when they've just gone to make a cup of tea?

It's funny how we've both properly settled down since we've moved to Brighton. I can't imagine myself doing that if I'd stayed in Buckinghamshire and carried on going out in London all the time. I was having too much fun.

STEPHEN

You and I were almost worse when we weren't dating, though. Chris turned into my mum and started telling me what to do. I bought my first ever car, a little yellow Mini, when I was 40, after finally passing my test. He phoned me up and shouted at me, telling me I should have got a cheaper car.

BOX CLEVER

CHRIS

Erm, looking back do you think I may have been right? You did scratch it up and knock one of the wing mirrors off. I feel a little bit safer in the car with Stephen now. He used to be such a bad driver his driving instructor had a stroke.

STEPHEN

That's true. During my second test my instructor sat in the back of the car. I drove round a roundabout too fast and mounted it. That was an instant fail and the examiner told me to go straight back to the test centre. My instructor was mortified.

I didn't hear from my instructor for a while so I phoned him at home to book in some more lessons. His wife answered and said, 'He's had a stroke and he doesn't want to teach you anymore.' I've definitely improved since then.

CHRIS

You do have every gadget possible on your car now, so you barely even drive it. It's even got auto drive.

STEPHEN

And it parks itself.

CHRIS

I'm a good driver but I do suffer from road rage. Inconsiderate drivers really piss me off. Stephen is always cutting people up and not realizing he's done it so people shout at him a lot.

STEPHEN

I got really beeped on the roundabout by Brighton Pier the other day. This cyclist was shouting at me saying, 'What the fuck are you doing? You're mental!' As I drove off I couldn't understand what I'd done, and the only thing I can think is that I went round the roundabout the wrong way. I also knocked a wing mirror off a lorry when I was driving through town and it made such a loud noise everyone turned round to look. I was stuck at a traffic light and I got really embarrassed so I pulled down the mirror and started doing my hair and acted really nonchalant. When the light turned green I sped off as if nothing had happened.

CHRIS

I got my first car, a Fiat X19, when I was 17 as an incentive to drive. I had it in my garage and I sneaked out and started the car before I'd even had a lesson and I tried to reverse it out. The garage was on a hill so the car started rolling backwards and I didn't know how to do a hill start. It crept all the way down the hill and I was about to hit a fence when I put my foot on the accelerator. So instead of hitting the fence I zoomed forward at such speed I smashed into the garage wall.

BOX CLEVER

STEPHEN

I think when we both got nice new cars, that was the time when we realized our lives had changed. When we started filming series three the crew were outside Chris's house waiting for us and I turned up in a brand new Kia Sportage. Then Chris rolled up in a new Nissan Qashqai. I'd also opened a hair salon, Chris had started his own hairdressing business from home, and then the show won a bloody BAFTA.

CHRIS

Little things started happening which made me realize my life had changed. I went and stayed in a hotel and they automatically upgraded me because the people working on reception were *Gogglebox* fans. I also booked to go and see *Les Miserables* in London and the only seats they had left online were really terrible. When I got to the theatre I went to the box office and said, 'Is there a possibility of paying for some better seats because this is all that was left?' They gave me the best seats in the house. I couldn't believe it.

STEPHEN

It's ridiculous, isn't it? We went to see the *Dreamboys* and they put us in a box at the side of the stage. All the other boxes were empty and it was weird that everyone was bending over backwards for us. They brought our drinks to the box and every time we went to the loo we got mobbed.

CHRIS

Stephen stayed in the box because it was all too hectic, but then people started coming round to the front of the box and leaning in to get photos. It was mad.

I think people feel like they know us from the show, but they only really get glimpses into our lives. We get to meet so many people we might otherwise not have met but sometimes when people are drunk they can act quite strangely. I was sat watching *The Lady Boys of Bangkok* in Brighton and this drunk lady came and sat on my lap and bellowed, 'Can you tell me about *Gogglebox*?' I was a bit like, 'Erm, I'm watching the show!'

There is the odd time when getting recognized is tricky but most of the time we're really happy to chat and do pictures.

Someone asked me the other day if I consider myself to be famous and I suppose we are in a way because we're on TV and people know us, but we're not *celebrities*. We're not falling out of nightclubs and dating TV presenters.

STEPHEN

I must admit that I prepare myself when I'm going somewhere now, and I factor in a bit of extra time in case people want to chat. That makes me sound like such a twat!

BOX CLEVER

CHRIS

I'm the same. Sometimes I have to give myself a bit of a pep talk and I have to build myself up to go out. I have days where I'm feeling a bit tired or down and I just want to hide away, but people are always lovely.

STEPHEN

I went through a phase of being a bit panicky when I went out and thinking someone may have a go at me. That's always in the back of my mind. And I do feel like when I speak to people there's pressure to be funny. I had a lady who came in the salon to get her hair done and after she'd finished she said, 'Oh, I thought you were going to be funnier,' and I was like, 'I'm doing your hair, not fucking stand up.'

CHRIS

The thing is, no one gets on with everyone and someone may catch you when you're having a really bad day and then they'll go and tell their mates you're an arsehole. But you've just got to go with it and be as nice as you can be. I usually let other people do all the talking.

I felt really bad for Stephen because he told me about this hair show he was going to in London a while ago. I said he was crazy, but he still went and he spent the whole day taking pictures with people and didn't get to see any of the stalls. At the end of the day he went to get a drink at the bar and a very drunk girl came over and said, 'Can I have a photo done with you?'

STEPHEN

I'd literally just got to the front of the queue and I was about to order so I said to her, 'Oh, love, I'm just about to get a drink. Can I do it in a bit?' She said, 'Fuck you then,' and stormed off. Sorry, whoever you are, but I couldn't risk missing out on my wine.

CHRIS

Nothing in our everyday lives has really changed. We both still work full-time and pop down to the supermarket to buy our bread and milk. I think there was a brief moment where we both let things run away with us a little bit and we thought we were going to be celebrities, but then we reined it in and realized it isn't about that.

STEPHEN

The producers have let us go off and do other things but they've done a really good job of keeping us all as non-celebrity as they can. And I don't think anyone sees us as celebrities. We're not in magazines every week or going to premieres.

I think the longer you're doing something the more grounded you become. Well, we did anyway. We've both got our feet firmly planted on the ground. We know that this is all going to end one day and I'm still going to have to cut hair for a living.

I think even if I hadn't been on the show Daniel and I would still have worked towards getting a salon together, which we have done, and I still would have done everything I wanted to. It just would have been a slower process and it wouldn't have been as easy without the extra money. Being on *Gogglebox* made things easier and life is more comfortable.

CHRIS

I don't think much about 'me' as a person has changed.

STEPHEN

Apart from the fact you're now dripping in Louis Vuitton.

CHRIS

Well, yes. I do have a few more nice designer bits. They're things I would have dreamt of buying before and I can afford some of them now. But I'm still careful.

I'm quite frugal with a lot of things but I'll go and spend £500 on a bag and a pair of shoes. I paid £200 for an umbrella recently, and my sunglasses were £400. But I really look after my stuff and I'm very careful.

STEPHEN

I look after my stuff for about the first week and then it ends up all over the place. I'd definitely leave an expensive umbrella on a train or something. I nearly bought some expensive sunglasses the other day and then I thought, 'Why? I'll only sit on them or something. I don't *need* them.'

CHRIS

I will treat myself to things I really love but I still like to use a lot of coupons and save money. Why would you pay full price for something you can get cheaper somewhere else? And I make sure I use all my store loyalty cards every time I shop.

STEPHEN

I don't own a single club card. I worry that if I started I'd end up with loads. They're so annoying. I'm not interested in any of them. My wallet would be full of shit.

People always say that to save money you should write down everything you spend. How is that going to save you money?

CHRIS

My best saving tip is don't leave the house if you're in a shopping mood. And don't shop online or get a credit card. I don't own any credit cards now. And don't ever go shopping for food when you're hungry because you'll buy so much crap you don't need and you don't end up eating it.

STEPHEN

But on the flip side, if you go when you're full you don't end up buying anything. You have to time it just right.

CHRIS

I learnt a lot about saving money from my mum when I was growing up, which has come in really useful. The other thing my mum taught me is not to shit on your own doorstep. And don't hang on to friendships that aren't good for you.

STEPHEN

The best advice my mum ever gave me was 'don't get caught'.

CHRIS

My mum had a real knack for making my friends feel uncomfortable when I was young. I'd have mates round and she'd walk into the living room and say to them, 'Have you taken root?' or, 'Haven't you gone home yet?' She was so blunt.

STEPHEN

We had an open-house policy in our house. Anyone was welcome at any time and our back door was never locked. People used to walk through our kitchen into the lounge and mum would shout, 'Make me a coffee!' without even turning round. Some people would automatically put the kettle on as soon as they walked in.

Everyone loved my mum because she used to let you smoke in the house and swear. My mates knew they could get away with stuff in my house.

CHRIS

Marie's friends got my mum stoned once. It was terrible. She had a panic attack and we had to call an ambulance for her. This paramedic was leaning on our lounge cabinet saying, 'What do you think brought the attack on?' and there was a rolled-up joint right next to him. Thankfully he didn't spot it, and my mum never tried a joint again.

STEPHEN

My mum tried a joint when I was about 14 and she said it didn't do anything for her. Then when she went to bed she had a dream that there were boxes all around her bedroom, and every time she opened one it was full of shitty knickers.

CHRIS

Our mums have met before and my mum was really chatty and Stephen's was really grumpy.

BOX CLEVER

STEPHEN

I know. It was because we all met up in a pub and the ceilings were too low for her. *And* it was too noisy even though there was no music on. It also didn't help that it was Boxing Day so it was really busy and she's not very good with big groups.

CHRIS

She isn't, is she? She is lovely but you're best off getting her when she's on her own. Every time Stephen pulls up outside my house with his mum in the car I'll give her a nice wave from the front door and she'll stick her middle finger up at me. She's hilarious.

STEPHEN

My mum is funny. She makes me laugh so much without even meaning to. I think other people think she's a bit mad but I find her hysterical.

Your mum is funny too. When we were in the pub that day she was drinking a sherry and she wanted to try some of my rosé wine. I said to her, 'I'll get you a glass, Doreen,' and she held up her half-full sherry glass and said, 'Don't worry, just pour it in there.'

CHRIS

My mum loves a sherry. I buy her a bottle of Harveys Bristol Cream for her birthday and Christmas every year. But she won't share it with anyone; that's *her* bottle. She'll have one on special occasions, or if she's really enjoying *EastEnders* one night. And at Christmas, of course.

STEPHEN

I love treating my family. It's nice to be able to go into a supermarket and not look at the price of absolutely everything. If I want to get a nice bottle of wine I don't automatically look at the bottom shelf anymore. That does feel like a bit of a luxury to be honest.

CHRIS

I do still look at price tags and I would never take anything for granted. I still have savings and my dream is to be mortgage-free in the next five to ten years.

STEPHEN

Oh, me too. Now I'm in my forties I've started earning good money and I'm definitely being more sensible. It's funny because I never panicked, even when I was really broke. I always knew everything would be alright. I always had this sense that it would work out so I lived life to the full.

I'd like to be mortgage-free by 55. I'd be happy to have a little part-time job and spend the rest of the time watching *Judge Judy*. That would do me. But in order to be able to do that I have to be sensible.

I tried on these amazing £500 sunglasses the other day and

I couldn't bring myself to buy them. I want to save money for the future. We're not stupid; we know this isn't how it's always going to be. Daniel's dad said to us recently, 'You're in the prime of your life and you're earning good money but don't make the mistake of thinking it's always going to be there, because it's not.' I've got my head together and I've got a plan.

CHRIS

I'd like to retire and travel around Europe in a caravan. I love caravanning. My friend Julia got a caravan based in Spain and it's in storage a lot of the year and then the rest of the time she rents a space in a caravan park and it's so cheap.

You meet some really lovely people in the park and everyone's living a nice, simple life. I've got all this 'stuff' around me I have to worry about. And the more I have, the more I worry. When I went on holiday I hid my wallet and my bag and my jewellery and I felt like I couldn't enjoy having them.

All you think about when you're caravanning is getting up, having breakfast and then going down to chill out by the pool. Then you maybe get lunch and go to the beach. What a great life!

I don't mind working hard – and I do work hard now, often six days a week – but that's fine because ultimately I'm working towards a goal of early retirement.

STEPHEN

I had a night in a caravan recently and I didn't mind it.

CHRIS

Daniel cried, didn't he?

STEPHEN

He wasn't keen. I would quite happily buy a plot of land and have a static mobile home built on it. I'd brick it all up around the bottom so it looked like a house but he's not having any of it.

In order not to have neighbours I would definitely go and live in a field in a static caravan. As long as it had running water. You can have hot showers in my friend's one. They're not like they were all those years ago when they smelt of mould and rust.

CHRIS

I'd love to see you on a caravanning holiday.

STEPHEN

I don't think it's for me, but I'd quite happily follow my mum's lead and go to India for six months every year like she did.

CHRIS

You look after your mum so well. We won't have kids who can do that. I think that's why I've always been so obsessed with doing well and setting myself up for the future.

BOX CLEVER

STEPHEN

I invest a lot in my goddaughter and I said to her the other day, 'You'd better come and see me when I'm old.' She's only three, but she'll owe me big time.

CHRIS

Having children never crossed my mind. All Marie ever went on about when we were growing up was having kids, but it never even entered my head. I always thought I'd get to a certain age and have a career and a house, and that was more important to me. I was always thinking about my future. I bought my first place when I was 22 and all my friends thought I was mad but some of them are still renting now. I was still going out and partying but I wanted that security behind me so I was sensible about stuff.

STEPHEN

Definitely no kids for me.

CHRIS

I like designer bags too much. I'd rather spend my money in Hugo Boss or Dolce and Gabbana. I hope that doesn't sound like I'm being a massive show off because that's not me at all. We've never tried to be anything other than ourselves.

I don't worry about what people think of us now. I did at first and now it's kind of faded because all I can do is be me and if people like me, then great.

STEPHEN

We met Rylan at the Specsavers Awards in 2014 – when I won the best newcomer award, thank you very much – and he said to us, 'Just be nice to everyone.' And that's what we do. We're nice people anyway but I guess we just have to make more of an effort at times.

CHRIS

We've met some amazing celebrities. Olivia Colman was so lovely to us. I've loved her since she did *Peep Show* and *Beautiful People* and I spotted her at an awards do last year. Stephen said I wasn't allowed to go over and speak to her but I *had* to, and she was so sweet.

STEPHEN

Christopher Biggins is great as well. At the Specsavers Awards Rylan and Gok Wan both told the audience they fancied Larry Lamb, so when I collected my award for best newcomer I said, 'I don't know why everyone is going on about Larry Lamb, I've got my eye on Christopher Biggins.' He was sat right by the side of the stage as I walked off so I kissed him! His partner, Neil, was sat next to him and it was all a bit of a laugh.

I told the story to *Heat* magazine during an interview and loads of other magazines picked up on it and made it out to be this big thing. I felt really bad on Biggins but he had given Chris his number so I got Chris to text him and say,

'I really hope you don't mind.' He replied straight away and said, 'Of course not darling, it was wonderful! Neil and I laughed and laughed.'

CHRIS

The last thing we wanted to do was offend Biggins and we didn't want him to think we'd planted a story to get press attention using his name. That would be our worst nightmare. He was brilliant about it, though.

STEPHEN

We've been lucky enough to meet some real icons like Biggins, Babs Windsor and Bruce Forsyth.

CHRIS

Pam St Clement, aka Pat from *EastEnders*, was very pleasant. We met her at a party for the Not Forgotten Association at Buckingham Palace two years ago.

STEPHEN

Sometimes celebs recognize us and approach us, and that's ridiculous. Nigel Planer from *The Young Ones* introduced himself to us at a party and told us he thought we were great on *Gogglebox*.

I was really excited and I said to him, 'Sometimes when I go round to Chris's I bang on the door and shout through the letterbox, "Open up, it's the piiiiiiiigs."' That was one of his classic lines from *The Young Ones* but I'm not sure he remembered it because he looked really confused.

CHRIS

We were having a right laugh with Nigel. We were surprised by how quiet Louie Spence and Graham Norton were when we met them. They were both absolutely lovely, but I think I was expecting them to be much more outgoing.

STEPHEN

Gok Wan wasn't that friendly to us.

CHRIS

Well you did call him fat on the show once, Stephen.

STEPHEN

I know. I do say bad things sometimes. I love the way kids just say what they think. Their brutal honestly is brilliant. At what age do you stop saying what you think and start worrying about offending people?

I think you start thinking about what you say more in your teens and then you stop giving a shit again when you're about 60. My mum tells people whatever she's thinking to your face. No holds barred. I heard my mum say to some woman the other day, 'You wanna cut that hair off, love. It looks manky.' To be fair, she was right.

BOX CLEVER

CHRIS

We all worry too much about being PC these days. I'm not saying we should go around offending people and being rude but everyone is constantly on alert. If a celebrity says something even slightly controversial it gets taken out of context and splashed all over the papers. I mean, look at what happened when Victoria Beckham posted that lovely photo of her kissing her daughter Harper on Instagram. People were going mad about it and calling her all sorts of names. It was pathetic. It was just a beautiful moment between a mum and daughter. If she'd been smacking Harper on the bum it would probably have got less coverage,

Celebrity culture is such a strange thing now. Back in the day people were on TV because they mixed in the right circles or they had a talent. Now someone who puts up a couple of posts on YouTube can become famous.

STEPHEN

It's different for us because we come from a generation that remembers the greats like Joan Collins and Diana Dors. You don't get those really glamorous women now.

These days everyone has come from a reality show. And I know we can't bloody talk. It's not like we're famous for our amazing musical talent or incredible acting skills.

I really like some reality TV, but some of it's so repetitive. It's all about doing up houses, cookery or fashion. Although I love anything with Sarah Beeny in it.

CHRIS

But we've always wanted to sort her hair out, haven't we?

STEPHEN

Yeah, because she's always got these really thick, chunky highlights and she's had the same style for years. She's got those three leather jackets she wears in rotation; the green one, the pink one and the blue one. It's the same boxy jacket but in different colours. And she's always pregnant.

CHRIS

I can understand why though because her husband is *fit*.

STEPHEN

What really bugs me is that *everything's* got a judging panel now.

CHRIS

There are even shows about knitting and sewing.

STEPHEN

The weirdest show was *The Big Painting Challenge* where they teamed up Richard Bacon and Una Stubbs to present it. She's so small she was nestling into his armpit. What a weird pairing.

BOX CLEVER

CHRIS

I can watch episodes of *Frasier* over and over again. I always see the beginning of them in the morning and then I have clients arriving so I never get to see the end and it really pisses me off. I've started to series link them now. Although I had so many on there I had to delete them because they were taking up too much room.

STEPHEN

Quiz question: which show has the most episodes, *Friends* or *Frasier*?

CHRIS

I reckon it was *Frasier*.

STEPHEN

It was, by one series. I was really surprised. I do like *Friends* but to me it's really obvious comedy.

CHRIS

We loved them all though.

STEPHEN

I didn't like Joey or Chandler. I just didn't think he was funny. I thought Rachel's character was hilarious, and I liked Monica.

CHRIS

I always thought I was most like Rachel.

STEPHEN

I thought Ross was funniest out of the blokes.

CHRIS

The girls were much better than the boys. One of my favourite shows now is *Millionaire Matchmaker*. And I loved *Desperate Housewives*.

STEPHEN

Eurgh, I hated it. *Hated* it. None of their faces moved and the ginger one drove me mad.

CHRIS

Bree?

STEPHEN

Yeah. Who gets named after cheese? Why not call her Cheddar or Stilton?

CHRIS

The stories were fantastic.

STEPHEN

I loved *Mork and Mindy* as a kid.

BOX CLEVER

CHRIS

When I was at primary school Sharon and I always watched *Laverne and Shirley* each morning with our coats on and then we'd have to run all the way to school to get there on time. That was in the days before you could push a button to record. We didn't get a video for years.

STEPHEN

And we only had four channels so to be fair we didn't really need one. I loved *Worzel Gummidge* too, with his thinking head.

CHRIS

I like *The Apprentice* because I love all the challenges. They all talk the talk but they're all shit.

STEPHEN

I do like *The X Factor* but I find the judging panel a bit annoying. I'm glad Dermot's back on it but is that a bit of a step back for him?

CHRIS

It would be like us going back to work at Toni and Guy? But apparently he's being paid a bloody fortune so I can see why he's doing it. And they had to try and improve on last year's. That judging panel was dreadful.

They make it too much about the judges generally. It

takes about half an hour before you get to hear someone sing because they're focusing on the judges so much. They all walk onto the stage and stand there like some kind of gods who are saving the world, and then we have to listen to loads of banter between them all before we even see a contestant. It's meant to be about the talent.

It's weird because now someone who's been a contestant on *The X Factor* and not done very well can build a career off the back of it, but quite often the people who do win don't do very well. It really is so easy to be in the public eye now.

I can't stand it when kiss-and-tell girls become famous. Rebecca Loos got in the papers because she supposedly slept with someone else's husband, and I think that's so wrong.

STEPHEN

Don't forget she also wanked a pig off on that TV show as well. She may have cheapened herself for a while but she managed to buy herself a four-bedroomed house in Kensington. I think if I was a girl and I had the opportunity to do what she did I would. Fuck it.

CHRIS

I cannot *stand* the Kardashians. They only got famous because of Kim's sex tape. I cannot believe that someone like Kim Kardashian has such an influence over the youth of today.

What's she got to teach people? How to have a big bum? It's so weird how some women are obsessed with having big arses now. Women are having fat sucked out of their guts and put into their bums.

I don't have any interest in any of that family. They're all beautiful in their own way and Kylie and Kendall are gorgeous, but I wish young girls had better role models.

STEPHEN

I just don't get them.

CHRIS

One thing I can't abide is showmances. It makes me so angry when these faux couples drag it out forever. They do it on all reality shows all the time now and it's so obvious. It's *so* boring.

STEPHEN

It bugs me what 'celebs' get paid for these days too. Josie Cunningham is the worst. She got famous for having a boob job on the bloody NHS. Why do magazines still feature her? Stop feeding into it!

CHRIS

I've got some really weird celebrity crushes. I've got a thing for Monty Don. It's his lovely big hands. He looks like he'd know what do with them. I had a selfie taken with him at the Hampton Court Flower Show in July and I was over the moon. I like a man who's good in the garden.

STEPHEN

That's why you like Tony – because he's a gardener.

CHRIS

I've always fancied Shayne Ward as well.

STEPHEN

No, he's all shiny.

CHRIS

I met him at an event and he was lovely. And really handsome.

STEPHEN

I fancy Burt Reynolds, and I also like the guy who played Ronnie Biggs in *Mrs Biggs*.

CHRIS

Daniel Mays? He was a right bastard in *Line of Duty*.

STEPHEN

There's something really sexy about him. I think it might be the cockney accent. I liked Noel Edmonds when I was younger. He was alright when he was in his twenties and thirties.

BOX CLEVER

CHRIS

Was it his blow-waved hair? Did you love his bouffant? I do love a man with a derma-wave. If you fancied him you must have liked all the Bee Gees because they all looked like him.

I'd say my weirdest crush is Sheldon from *The Big Bang Theory*. I think it's because he's really clever. I also fancy Eric Cantona and Sacha Baron Cohen.

Arrogance is a real-turn off for me. I do like confidence and I like a man who can walk into a room and you notice him, but I don't like it when guys are full of themselves.

STEPHEN

I like a cheeky chappy.

CHRIS

This may sound weird but I had a real thing for Sam Fox when I was about ten. I thought she was beautiful.

STEPHEN

That does sound weird.

CHRIS

It was more of an admiration thing I think. I remember looking at her and thinking she was gorgeous and she had an amazing pair of knockers on her and I wanted to be like her. I loved her music as well. 'Touch Me' is one of the best songs ever.

STEPHEN

Sam did come across as lovely as well. Linda Lusardi seemed quite classy. But you could have had a nice cup of tea with Sam.

CHRIS

And a bit of Battenberg.

STEPHEN

Kathy Lloyd was beautiful as well. What a funny thing Page 3 was. They don't do it anymore, do they? Everyone protested against it?

CHRIS

If I were straight my ideal woman would be Charlize Theron. She's so beautiful. Especially in the J'Adore perfume advert.

STEPHEN

I thought you were going to say, 'Especially in *Monster*.'

CHRIS

Weirdo. I like a bit of Jennifer Aniston too. She's very girl next door. When I first met my ex, Nigel, and I was dressed up as Christina he told me I looked like her.

BOX CLEVER

STEPHEN

I'd go straight for a young Raquel Welch. She still looks amazing. It's probably not going to be amazing downstairs though, is it?

CHRIS

Faye Dunaway was stunning when she was younger but she looks like she's had a lot of work done now. Although she says she hasn't.

STEPHEN

That'll be us in 30 years' time.

Chapter Eight

RULES OF ENGAGEMENT

Stephen: 'I was scared of saying to someone, "Yes, this is it. We'll be together for the rest of our lives."'

STEPHEN

I definitely think my proper partying days are over now. I could never go back to going clubbing all night and existing on two hours' sleep. Now, unless I'm going to a special event, I like to be safely tucked up in bed before 11pm.

CHRIS

I'm the same. I used to be able to party non-stop. Now if I go to bed later than 1am I feel like I've got a hangover even if I haven't been drinking. I very rarely put myself in a position where I have a hangover. I'll have a few drinks but I don't go over the top.

I used to love a party. Vodka was always my favourite drink as a teenager when I could afford it. I remember going to the Grape and Grain off licence near my house when I was 18 and getting a little bottle of vodka for myself. I passed Sainsbury's and decided to go in and check if I could have got it cheaper in there. Yes, Stephen, even back then I was trying to save money.

My bottle was in my inside pocket and this old woman on the checkout must have seen it and thought I'd nicked it, so she sent the security guards after me. They chased me down the street and wrestled me to the ground accusing me of stealing. They were well embarrassed when they realized Sainsbury's didn't sell the brand I had.

I wasn't a massive drinker in my teens but I do remember lying on my bedroom floor drunk a few times, thinking I knew everything about the meaning of life.

STEPHEN

The best hangover cure for me is a full-fat Coke, a full English and a long walk with the dogs. Back in the clubbing days, I'd go for another drink the following day to sort myself out but I can't get away with that anymore.

CHRIS

God, I can barely eat the following day let alone have another drink. I used to take Resolve and that would sort me out but nothing works now.

STEPHEN

We do tend to get pissed at most of the PAs we do though. . .

A PA is basically where we get paid to turn up at a club and chat to people. They're bloody brilliant, but if we're doing one on a Wednesday night with a thousand 18-year-olds we have to have a few drinks.

Some people go mad when we arrive. To be fair, they've probably already had a ton of booze. We did a PA in Scotland recently and a load of girls were screaming for us. Two old gay men!

CHRIS

These days I'll drink a bit of rosé or a shandy, but I can't touch sambuca because Stephen and I had some in New York and it burnt my insides and made me feel bloody awful. I tried it again at the Specsavers Awards and it made me ill again.

STEPHEN

Oh God, what a night.

CHRIS

The next morning wasn't much fun though. I was being sick every five minutes in the hotel bathroom. See, it was the sambuca.

RULES OF ENGAGEMENT

STEPHEN

I went into the loo to have a poo and it suddenly occurred to me how funny it would be if I didn't flush it. I put the lid down really quietly and went back and laid on the bed.

After a few minutes Chris said, 'I'm going to be sick again,' and stumbled into the toilet. I ran in after him and watched him pick the lid up, scream and then throw up.

CHRIS

Bastard.

STEPHEN

I was on the floor laughing. It is honestly one of the funniest things I've ever seen.

CHRIS

I only got into that state because you were knocking back so much booze you were getting lairy and I knew I had to get drunk to get on the same level as you. I had to make myself numb so I could handle you.

STEPHEN

I think I heckled Gok Wan at some point.

CHRIS

And you seriously wonder why he's not very friendly towards you?

We ended up in a club in Soho after the awards. This group of guys recognized us so they paid for us to get in and bought us drinks all night. It was amazing.

We were doing all these stupid pretend sex moves on the dancefloor and some woman was taking loads of photos of us. God knows where they've ended up but I'm glad they haven't turned up on Twitter or anything.

We had to leave our hotel room by 10am and all I wanted to do was get home and go to bed. I honestly didn't know how I was going to handle the train journey.

Our hotel was in Trafalgar Square so we got into a taxi to Victoria station and I felt so shit I had to make the cab driver pull up so I could be sick. The nearest place he could stop was outside Buckingham Palace. I'm sorry, ma'am, but I vomited outside your house.

STEPHEN

While he was outside throwing up the taxi driver looked at me in his rear view mirror and said, 'Is he alright?' and I replied, 'Yeah, he's just a fucking lightweight.'

CHRIS

I got zero sympathy. I couldn't even keep water down. I was sick about three times on the train.

STEPHEN

He was weaving up and down our carriage trying to get to

the toilet and I was almost willing him to throw up over someone just because it would have made me laugh. I think I was still a bit drunk.

CHRIS

I was so relieved when I got home. I got my duvet, pulled it over my head and went to sleep for the rest of the day.

STEPHEN

I laid on the sofa for the rest of the day laughing about the poo. What a bitch.

CHRIS

There were a few times I went out and got horribly drunk as Christina and I looked at myself in the mirror and thought I looked a right state. I think that put me off drinking quite a bit. No one wants to be a sloppy drag queen.

One night when I was out as Christina I got very drunk. When I eventually got a taxi home I got the driver to drop me off at the bottom of the road. I was still with my ex-boyfriend Nigel at the time and he was always having a go at me for slamming cab doors outside the bedroom window.

I staggered up the street and fell over a recycling bin into someone's garden. I got back up and slapped my long blonde wig back on my head just as my neighbour, Father John, was leaving his house to go and open up the local church.

261

When I eventually got into my house the heels on my £200 boots were both bent from where I'd been stumbling about. I was so gutted I shrieked so loudly that I ended up waking Nigel up anyway.

STEPHEN

You were trash.

CHRIS

I know, I was *totally* trashed.

STEPHEN

No, you were *trash*.

CHRIS

I met Nigel when I was dressed as Christina. I was at a bar on the seafront about 15 years ago with the Toni and Guy lot, my friend Michelle and my ex, Greg. Michelle was tired so her and Greg went home. I went up to the bar to get a glass of water and this guy came up and wrapped his arms around me and said, 'You've got a lovely little body.' When I turned around he said, 'Oh, you're a *boy*,' and I replied, 'Is that a problem?' It turned out it wasn't.

This gorgeous man looked like George Clooney and I was so taken aback by him I think I went into a mild state of shock. I felt like I was in love with him from the moment I saw him.

RULES OF ENGAGEMENT

We stayed in contact after we broke up six-and-a-half years later, because we still cared about each other a lot and wanted to stay in each other's lives. As time went on our friendship grew stronger and stronger and now I wouldn't be without him for anything. It's really nice because Nigel and Tony get on brilliantly, and he's always popping round to ours for a cuppa and a chat, and he feeds my pussy when we go away.

STEPHEN

Why did you call yourself Christina? Your name's Chris. Couldn't you have gone for something more interesting?

CHRIS

I guess because she was a female version of me and if I'd been born a girl I maybe would have been called Christina instead of Christopher.

STEPHEN

I've done a lot of really bad drag over the years. My alter ego is called Loretta and she only came to life when I was in Ibiza a few years ago. I went out this one night wearing an American flag waterfall jacket with a matching mini skirt and platforms. I had a false pair of boobs on and this long peroxide blonde wig called Loretta, hence the name. My mate Ollie is a make-up artist and he did my make-up for me. I thought I looked amazing. Clearly I was very, very pissed.

CHRIS

I've always done *good* drag and Stephen's always done *bad* drag. Some people just do it for a laugh and because you can be really outrageous, but I didn't start doing it so I could wear gigantic wigs and long sequined dresses. I didn't want to look like Widow Twankey and make it into a comedy thing. I took Christina really seriously. I've always seen myself as a gender illusionist because quite often people couldn't work out what sex I was.

STEPHEN

I think you could definitely still get away with being Christina now. I think you'd look even better because you carry yourself so well and you've got a bit more money so you'd have better clothes.

CHRIS

My wigs were always really good. Even if I was skint I'd find the money for them. They were £500 wigs and I used to spend about £100 on extensions to bulk them out. If you've got a cheap wig people will spot it a mile off. It's the biggest giveaway.

I was never nervous about going out dressed as Christina because she gave me something to hide behind. I was more nervous being myself back then.

RULES OF ENGAGEMENT

STEPHEN

You probably looked easy.

CHRIS

I looked classy! Actually, I looked beautiful.

STEPHEN

Every time I saw you out dressed as Christina you looked like a slut. You used to go out in high heels, a mini skirt and a bikini top. That doesn't scream *demure*. The way you walked didn't help.

CHRIS

I didn't walk, I *sashayed*. When you're a gay man there's a lot of pressure to look masculine on the scene. If you're feminine in any way it can be frowned upon. And there was me dressing up as a bloody woman. I don't think all the gay guys I met approved.

But then I got to a point in my mid thirties where I didn't want to look like a desperate old hag. I think you should do what you can to the best of your ability and then walk away when it's not working for you anymore. And there came a point when I knew it was time to hang up my heels.

Rather than trying to eek it out for a few more years when the cracks in the foundation appear, you should bow out gracefully. And I did. I never wanted to be that person people looked at and thought, 'Gawd, she's seen better days.'

STEPHEN

You still dress up occasionally don't you? You did go out dressed as Conchita Wurst a few years back?

CHRIS

I did. I dressed up as her for a Eurovision party and I absolutely adored it. It was an opportunity to do it without having to shave my beard off.

The only problem is that now if I wanted to be Christina for a night again, I wouldn't want to shave my beard off. I've had it for years and I hate the idea of being without it for two weeks while it grows back.

I really thought that was the one night I wouldn't get recognized but people still came up to me and said, 'You look fabulous. And I love you on *Gogglebox*.'

The thing is, I was dressing up so much at one point in my life because I was so unhappy with myself as a male, and I don't feel like that anymore. I was losing myself in the character of Christina and in the end I felt like it was becoming unhealthy. I knew that if I was going to stop being 'her' I had to go cold turkey because there wasn't anything left of the real me that I liked.

When I was younger, if I was feeling really shit and under-confident I could dress myself up as Christina and I was sorted. When I walked into a room everyone wanted to talk to 'Christina' and everyone would flock to me. So I kept hiding behind this person that made me feel really good.

But the downside of that was that I started to fade as a person. As *Chris*. I loved Christina but I also resented her because I wanted to feel that confident when I was just myself. And instead I felt like crap.

I got to a point where I knew that if I wanted to meet a guy I could settle down with and be happy with I'd have to start living my life as myself full time. I had no problem pulling when I was dressed up but it was a novelty, and none of the guys I met wanted to get to know me as a person. They just wanted to go to bed with Christina and be able to tell their mates about it. Some guys even wanted me to pretend to be their girlfriend full-time. How was that going to work? I wasn't trans, and there's no way I could dress up every day when I had a job and a life away from that world.

One of the turning points for me was when this guy I'd known for a while told me he really fancied me as Christina but not as Chris. He was a gay guy and he still only wanted to sleep with me when I was dressed as a girl. I was the same person with the same body; I just had different hair and tits strapped on. It started to become really confusing for me *as well as* people around me.

Sometimes I'd say hello to people in bars I'd met when

I'd been dressed up and they didn't have a clue who I was. They always looked a bit let down when they realized. People often said, 'Oh, I love Christina. Why isn't she coming out tonight?' as if she really was a totally different person.

I had to stop doing Christina and start living as myself, and it took me to the age of 35 to do that. That's when I realized I wanted to start being authentic. I also basically had to learn to like myself again because I had been hiding behind an alter ego for so long I had totally lost sight of the real me. I wanted to find out how much of me there was in Christina, and who I could be if I let her go.

I started going to the gym and being more boyish, but that brought up a whole new set of problems because then I started to obsess about being buff and perfect. Everywhere I looked all these guys looked so muscular and I felt inferior next to them. Obviously that wasn't the reality, but it gave me a whole new way to put myself down.

It took me until I'd stopped doing Christina for about a year to realize I'm not actually that bad. I was so hung on what other people were thinking and their opinions of me and I had to really push myself to let that go.

Brilliantly, these days I just don't care. I've still got issues like everyone else, but liking myself isn't one of them. In a way Christina helped me to work out who I am, after years of trying to make myself popular by putting on an act.

RULES OF ENGAGEMENT

STEPHEN

And you grew up and matured around that time too. We all do that, and we start seeing things differently. You've learnt to deal with being a gay man now, and in my opinion you've never looked better.

I've never really been through a phase of not really knowing who I was but I've had my hang ups. I've always thought I've got a fat belly. Now I look back at photos of me in my twenties and I think, 'Oh my God, I wish I looked like that now'.

CHRIS

You are obsessed with your belly, but there are always things we don't like about ourselves. You've never been short on confidence.

STEPHEN

I always thought I was alright looking and I've never had a problem pulling.

CHRIS

Every drag queen has to have a dramatic ending and Christina was no different. When I stopped dressing up people used to say, 'I haven't seen Christina in a while,' and I'd tell them she went over Beachy Head in her pink Mercedes convertible.

I made up a whole story about how she'd swerved because she saw a rabbit in the road. Some people speculated that she swerved because she wanted to turn the rabbit into some nice warm gloves for winter, but I know she would never have done that because she was an animal lover.

As a result of having to swerve, Christina sped off Beachy Head and Fifi, her faithful poodle, jumped out of the car just in time to save herself. Fifi was found by a hiker a couple of hours later, peering over the edge of the cliff and howling.

Christina's car was hoisted up by the emergency services but no body was found, and to this day her whereabouts remain a mystery.

Some people have speculated that she was found alive by someone who has whisked her off to Switzerland so she can go into hiding, and they're rebuilding her face so she can come back looking even more beautiful than before. Other people say she's still at Beachy Head, hanging on the cliff face for dear life. And some really mean people say she was eaten by sharks. But we all know there are no sharks in British waters.

Maybe one day we'll find out what *really* happened to her. She may even make a big comeback. For the right money, obviously.

STEPHEN

Maybe she could try and launch a pop career? I reckon she could be the new Britney. But with a better weave.

I started to get properly into music when I was about eleven. Our babysitter, Sheena, gave me some money for my birthday and I walked to Woolworths to buy my first ever single – Blondie's 'The Tide is High'. When I got to the music section I saw that Abba were at number one with 'Super Trouper' and I had a right panic. I got so flustered I ended up buying Abba instead and I still regret it to this day.

CHRIS

I think you made the right choice. I grew up listening to Abba. We had a really old-fashioned gramophone and we used to sit around it and listen to Abba and The Carpenters. We'd all dance around the living room together and they're my first real memories of music.

The first single I ever bought was 'Brother Louie' by Modern Talking and I've still got it to this day.

STEPHEN

I was more into soul music than pop. I liked artists like Gwen Guthrie, Alexander O'Neal and Whitney Houston.

CHRIS

You love your Whitney, don't you?

STEPHEN

I was a massive fan. And I liked Aretha Franklin and Dionne Warwick. Do you remember Princess's song 'Say I'm Your Number One'? That was a classic.

I hated Madonna growing up. I thought she was slutty. I

was all about Whitney. I'm probably the only gay man in the world who didn't like her. Whitney was glamorous and pure, whereas Madonna was always grabbing her bits on stage.

CHRIS

I loved the charts and I absolutely loved music videos. We were the third family on the estate to get Sky and I thought MTV was *amazing*. I probably spent about half my teenage years watching it.

STEPHEN

Did you know that Whitney Houston was the first black woman to appear on MTV?

CHRIS

I didn't, but that's a good fact. MTV opened to my eyes to a much wider variety of music. I was really into a glam rock band called Vixen for a while. Then I discovered this Swedish group in my teens called Army of Lovers and I was completely obsessed by them. They really dressed up and looked so over the top and I wanted my hair and make-up just like theirs. I was already a bit of a freak at that point so I thought if I ever met them they'd 'get' me.

STEPHEN

I loved Adam and the Ants. And I loved them more than ever when Diana Dors was in the video for 'Prince Charming'.

RULES OF ENGAGEMENT

I never buy music anymore. I used to listen to Radio 2 and now I've progressed to Radio 4. I like to hear people talking when I'm driving, not loads of thumping.

CHRIS

You sound like such a grumpy old man. I think it depends on what you're doing. If you're getting ready to go on a night out it's good to have some up-tempo stuff on. My music collection is really varied and I have everything from opera to dance music to Celtic Woman on my iPod. I like a bit of Rihanna and Katy Perry and that sort of thing too.

STEPHEN

What the fuck is Celtic Woman? I think all the Rihannas and Katys and Taylors sound the same. My mates all used to call you Rihanna when we first started dating because you danced to her one of her songs like a lunatic when we were out one night. Do you remember that?

CHRIS

I do. They were probably jealous of my moves. At the end of the day you can't beat a bit of Barbra Streisand. She has a song for every mood. If you're feeling sad? Listen to Barbra? If you're feeling happy? Whack on Barbra. If you're going for a night out? Barbra's got the tunes to get you in the mood.

WE NEED TO TALK

STEPHEN

You and I always used to do Barbra and Donna Summer on karaoke. 'Enough is Enough' was our tune.

CHRIS

We used to kill it. And not in a good way. I'm *such* a Babs fan.

STEPHEN

You've got her nose. I reckon if you dragged up as her you'd look like her.

CHRIS

I would. I'd do that classic look where she's wearing a turban and looks fabulous. The last time I counted I had about 58 Babs albums.

STEPHEN

I had a really good dance routine to Mai Tai's 'Our Love is History'.

CHRIS

I loved Kylie from the moment she released her first single. Sharon would be sitting in her room blasting out New Kids on the Block and I'd be in my room blasting out Kylie. We had proper music wars and we had some huge rows about who was better. I was so passionate about Kylie I still feel quite angry about it. Where are New Kids on the Block now? Nowhere. Where's Kylie? Still going strong.

STEPHEN

I reckon the best time for me musically was around '89 when house music was just starting to break through. I loved all that. I don't like that much modern music, but I do think Adele is amazing.

God, do you remember when we met Example at Pride in Birmingham and we nicked a bottle of champagne from his dressing room while he was on stage? We only had a swig each and then we hid it behind a filing cabinet because we were scared of getting caught.

CHRIS

I don't think he liked us much. I was really into films as a kid too. I was mad on the movie *Ghost* and I thought it was so romantic.

STEPHEN

I loved *Mannequin, Weird Science* and *The Breakfast Club*.

CHRIS

Pretty in Pink was brilliant. Molly Ringwald was a massive star when we were kids, then all of a sudden she disappeared.

STEPHEN

Dirty Dancing was such a great film too.

CHRIS

Grease was always on in our house. I must have watched it about a hundred times thanks to my sisters.

STEPHEN

My sister Denise went to see it every night for ten nights. *Footloose* was amazing. And of course we got to work with Kevin Bacon on the EE advert, which was surreal. He was such a nice guy. We got flown out to New York to film that and it was bloody brilliant.

CHRIS

Flight of the Navigator is another classic movie. And *Jaws*, *Poltergeist* and *The Last House on the Left*. All the Freddy Krueger movies were horrific. I used to sit behind the sofa whenever my sisters hired out any *Nightmare on Elm Street* films. I also saw a film called *The Entity* that scared me shitless.

STEPHEN

My favourite kids' film ever is *The Amazing Mr Blunden*. It's a Christmas ghost story and Diana Dors is in it. It's amazing. Do you think I'm a bit fixated on Diana Dors?

RULES OF ENGAGEMENT

CHRIS

My favourite movie of all time – and probably the only thing in the world that makes me shed a tear – is *Somewhere in Time*. It's a love story with Christopher Reeve and Jane Seymour and it's so moving.

I made Tony watch it and he was really surprised about how upset I got because he doesn't usually see me like that.

STEPHEN

Have you ever seen *Who Will Love My Children?* We watched it as a family and we were all in floods of tears.

CHRIS

I must admit, that did touch me.

STEPHEN

Did it now? Did you ever see the 'Confessions' movies? Like *Confessions of a Window Cleaner?* They were proper soft porn. And the *Carry On* films too. I thought they were filth when I was a kid. I love chick flicks now. I find *Bridesmaids* hysterical. I do love a wedding.

So many chick flicks are about weddings. The best part of a wedding for me is always the speeches. I've done two in my life and both times I spent two weeks walking around the house reading them out aloud. I'd stop for the punchline so people could laugh and everything.

My biggest achievements in my life so far are getting engaged to Daniel, washing elephants in India, climbing to Mount Everest Base Camp, and giving my sister Beverley away on her wedding day.

CHRIS

Well you couldn't sell her.

STEPHEN

I wish I could put that eye rolling emoji in here. Chris and I both got engaged around the same time. But Chris did do it first.

CHRIS

Yes, I was *first*. And it was a total surprise. Tony had always said that if he was going to ask me to marry him he'd do it at the bandstand in Brighton because it's his favourite land-mark. So, to be honest, when we arranged a trip to Paris Tony proposing didn't even cross my mind. I just thought it was a belated birthday present from the year before because we'd been talking about it for ages. We were waiting until Tony's flat sale went through and then he was going to treat us, but it turned out he'd been planning the whole thing for months and months.

I think Stephen suspected though. I remember us having a conversation when we were filming *Gogglebox* one night and he asked me if he thought Tony was going to pop the question while we were away. I made a joke and said, 'I doubt it, but if the rock's big I'll say yes.' Does that sound bad?

Tony claims I told him within a month of us meeting exactly how and where I wanted to get married, and I also told him not to bother proposing unless he had an amazing ring. I honestly don't remember saying all of that, but to be fair it does sound like something I would do.

It turned out Tony had planned every single bit of our break, right down to making me go through security at the Eiffel Tower before him. They do bag checks and he didn't want to be in front of me in case the security guards pulled out the engagement ring.

I could tell Tony was feeling nervous that day, but he's scared of heights so I just put it down to that. Then when we got to the top of the Tower he was really taking his time looking around, which surprised me. I thought he'd want to have a quick look around and then get back to ground level as soon as possible.

He suggested we took another photo and said he wanted to find someone to take a picture of us. I said we should just do a selfie, but it was too late – he'd already given his camera to some old man.

He started fumbling around in his bag and that's when it suddenly hit me. I know this is terrible, but one of the first things I thought was, 'What if I don't like the ring?'

STEPHEN

But it's not about the ring; it's about the sentiment behind it. Honestly, Chris.

CHRIS

It did go through my mind though! I also thought, 'Shit, am I ready for this?' I'm a bit of a commitment-phobe and even though I absolutely love Tony I've always had a bit of a fear of properly settling down.

It all happened so quickly and when Tony pulled out the ring I was like, 'Oh my God, it's amazing!' I thought it was the most beautiful ring I'd ever seen. He'd spent ages choosing it, bless him. He wanted a ring that looked like an engagement ring but wasn't too girlie. And it was *perfect*. It's a champagne diamond, which I love.

Obviously I said yes and then we had pink champagne to celebrate. Paris is the city of love so there isn't a better place to get engaged. It's always going to hold a special place in my heart.

We were in Paris for a few more days and we spent the time wandering around sightseeing and eating. It was so nice and relaxed and if I could go back and do it all again tomorrow, I would.

Stephen always said he didn't want to get married. Then one day he turned up at my place with an engagement ring for Daniel and told me he was going to propose when they were on holiday.

Rules of Engagement

STEPHEN

Like you, I was scared of saying to someone, 'Yes, this is it. We'll be together for the rest of our lives.'

I'd always been unsure about marriage, but I was sat in mine and Daniel's living room last Boxing Day and something came over me. We'd had such a nice Christmas together and I ended up driving into town there and then. I went to The Lanes and waited for all the jewellers to open. I looked through the window of the first shop I came to and my eyes looked straight at the ring I ended up buying.

Daniel and I were going on holiday to India a week later and I wanted to propose while we were out there. I had to transport the ring from Heathrow to Dubai, then from Dubai to Kerala, and then on to Delhi. I had the ring in my pocket the whole time and I was terrified I was going to lose it.

Daniel and I got picked up from Delhi airport in a big black Mercedes and we went straight to the Taj Palace Hotel to check in. It's seven star and it was so beautiful and the manager *and* the assistant manager came out to greet us. They took us directly up to the seventh floor without us even having to check in, and when got out of the lift a butler was stood there with two glasses of champagne.

That night we went downstairs to have dinner in the hotel restaurant. It was so posh every time one of our dishes came over the waiter carrying the tray would be flanked by two other waiters, and they'd both lift the cloches off at the same time.

It was really romantic and I thought about going upstairs to our room to get the ring, but there were only two other tables full of people in the restaurant so there wasn't much of an atmosphere.

My plan all along had been to do it at the Taj Mahal, so the following day we jumped into our swanky Mercedes and drove for three hours to get there. When we arrived it was absolutely heaving with people and I got recognized twice from *Gogglebox* so I spent ages chatting to some other British people. It just didn't feel special enough to do it there. It was too hectic and touristy so I suggested we went for a drink so we could have a breather.

We went to the incredible Oberoi hotel nearby, and it worked out perfectly. We popped for a drink on the balcony and the view was unbelievable. It overlooked these beautiful gardens and we could see the Taj Mahal in the distance.

I asked Daniel to take a picture of me and as he held up the camera I told him to zoom in. He could see I was holding something in my hand and he said, 'What is it? What is it?' When he finally realized he said, 'Oh my God!' and tears welled up in his eyes. I walked over to him and said, 'I really love you. Will you marry me?'

Just before we'd arrived in India the country backtracked on its gay rights laws and made it illegal, so Daniel and I couldn't do any big displays of affection in case we got handcuffed. Instead we had a quick cuddle and when the waiter came out he said, 'Celebrating something?' We were like, 'No, no!'

We went down into the Oberoi restaurant and had a lovely meal. We got the car back to our hotel and it wasn't until we were in the room that we could properly celebrate.

CHRIS

We don't need to know that.

STEPHEN

It meant a lot to me to propose in India. As I've mentioned, I spent a lot of time travelling around there when I was younger and that's where I really found out who I was, so it seemed really appropriate.

This sounds so unromantic but I just want to get the wedding done now.

We still don't know what we want to do. We did think about having it in my neighbour's garden because it's huge. You could probably fit about 200 in there. We were considering having an Indian-themed wedding with a marquee, and Daniel and I would be wearing Indian-style outfits. Then we thought we'd like to keep it quite small and maybe go to the south of France with 20 really close friends and hire a chateau.

I would quite happily run off somewhere and grab two witnesses off the street and just get it done but it's really important to Daniel to have his family there. I'm not overly fussed really. I'll probably end up doing whatever Daniel fancies. And let him organize it all.

CHRIS

I don't care what you do as long as I'm invited.

STEPHEN

You're not coming as bloody Christina.

I think the secret to a good relationship is being able to laugh with someone. My friend Melissa says that when she goes and stays with her parents, who are in their seventies, she still hears them chuckling when they go to bed at night. I think that's brilliant.

I'm quite old-fashioned when it comes to marriage in some ways. I do think that whatever you build when you're in a marriage should be shared. It's both of yours. It becomes 'ours'. There's no dividing things up.

Neither Daniel nor I had very much when we first met so we started on an equal footing. I feel like we've worked towards everything together.

CHRIS

Tony was married many, many years ago and he didn't do what he wanted, so he feels like he should have the wedding he's always dreamed of this time around. He wants it to be bigger and better. We've already booked The Grand in

Brighton for 80 people for our wedding next summer, and then lots more will come along in the evening. I'm a bit worried about how many we'll end up having. We keep thinking of more people we'd like to invite.

I've been having such a nightmare with my groomsmaids dresses. I found some I liked but they were £275 each and I need four of them. That's a lot of money for half a day. Everything associated with weddings seems to double in price, doesn't it? The minute you say 'wedding' people whack the prices up.

STEPHEN

I would rather spend our money on a decent buffet at a wedding than a sit down meal. I think they're boring. It's always a bit of salmon or chicken with a couple of boiled potatoes and some vegetables. It's never that great and all everyone wants to do is get stuck into the wine.

CHRIS

What you did for your engagement do was really nice.

STEPHEN

We had a lovely party in a bar in my village. The flowers were absolutely beautiful but they cost a fortune and once everyone was in the bar you couldn't see any of them.

We also paid for this busker to come and play. Daniel and I met her on one of our dates in London and she was amazing, but you couldn't hear her singing above the chatter. It was a shame.

I'm not bothered about having a massive stag do. I would like to take a handful of our friends out for dinner and get a bit pissed.

CHRIS

Shouldn't you have one of your own though? You're going to be spending the rest of your life with Daniel. I'm sure you can manage one night away from him?

What should we call it? Is it a stag or hen do? I might call mine a slag do. I'm planning to go away for a long weekend, or maybe even a week somewhere hot, and have a bloody good time. Without Tony, in the nicest possible way. If I'm going to be spending the rest of my life with someone I'm going to wave off my single years in style. With Stephen by my side.

THANK YOUS

Thank you to Tania Alexander, Harriet Manby, the lovely production and editing team and everyone else at the brilliant Studio Lambert for making *Gogglebox* the great show it is.

Thanks to Channel 4 for commissioning *Gogglebox* and helping to make it such a huge success.

Thanks to Ben Clark and everyone at the fantastic LAW.

Thanks to Holly Harris, Sarah Emsley, Liz Marvin and everyone at Headline for giving us the opportunity to get our story out there.

THANK YOUS

Thanks to photographer Pal Hansen and the rest of the team who worked on the cover shoot and made it such a fun day.

Thanks to Jeremy and Doreen for being such great hosts and letting Buddy and Rusty share your toys during our visits.

And a massive thank you to Jordan Paramor for doing such an amazing job of ghostwriting the book and being there to hand out tissues when we laughed and cried our way through the interviews.

And finally, a huge thank you goes to the delivery men of Brighton and Hove for being so prompt with our unhealthy takeaways. Your hard work is appreciated.